Praise for *TAKE ACTION! Revise Later*

"*TAKE ACTION! Revise Later* isn't just another book to add to your to-do list. It's a compact jump-start-your-business-and-get-it-rolling-full-steam-ahead-quick-reading-guide to making your business ideas a reality. Not only is it chock full of useful information, but Bob the Teacher provides inspiration and a fresh perspective on running your own business. The lessons he teaches are about getting going now. It's time to stop thinking and start doing—like reading this book today!"

Felicia J. Slattery, M.A., M.Ad.Ed.
Author of Cash in on Communication
CommunicationTransformation.com

"Whether you're just starting your business or have been in business for years, you should definitely run, not walk, to purchase *TAKE ACTION! Revise Later*. Success leaves clues and it's possible to model excellence by following the strategies outlined in this fabulous book. Why struggle on your journey when there's a resource so easily accessible that will shorten your learning curve, decrease your frustration and increase your chances of success?"

Kathy Santini
Success Coach, Educator and Speaker
SavvyAboutSuccess.com

"Clear, concise and of course, simple. Bob's lessons are like a pebble in a pool of clear water...the ripples will powerfully impact both your business and your life. And as a bonus, he gives you the steps to take action immediately. I don't know how he does it, but for the growth in my business, I'm just glad he did!"

Chris Makell, MS, CPC
Marketing and Radiant Profits Mentor
RadianceMarketing.com

"As one of Bob The Teacher's more 'mature' students, I didn't grow up with computers. It took me a while to appreciate the obvious sense of the *TARL* strategy. But had I waited for everything to be perfect to my eyes, my websites would still be in draft form and I would still be at the starting blocks. When I look back at my first attempts at online marketing I cringe, but using *TARL* I can easily change things even now. I wholeheartedly endorse the approach of *TAKE ACTION! Revise Later* as an essential for success in any business."

Bob Lampard
London, England
LaughingYourWayToLove.com

"*TAKE ACTION! Revise Later* gives you a practical and metaphorical kick in the butt, especially if you're a recovering perfectionist! Bob will you're your biggest objections and dismantle them down to their lowest common denominator – excuses. Have a copy of Bob's book handy for those days when you simply can't move forward. With each chapter, Bob throws you a proverbial life preserver, ensuring that life-as-we-know-it will not end if your website isn't perfect, your copy clean and your graphics flawless. After reading this book, you'll learn to forgive your foibles and cheer your successes – because you're finally in action, not simply planning for it."

Lisbeth A. Tanz
Freelancer Business Strategist and Professional Writer/Editor
SavvyFreelanceWriters.com

"Bob Jenkins has done it again! First an inspiration in the classroom and over the social media airwaves, Bob now brings his unique ability to transform the complex into common sense to book form. In *TAKE ACTION! Revise Later* Bob brilliantly breaks down the most dizzying concepts for building an online business into simple, digestible bites that are easy to swallow. But much more than that, he inspires a wonderful sense of self-confidence because his lessons are so very memorable."

Kim Nishida
ProfitableCommunities.com

"Save yourself 3 years of trial and error and absorb everything you can from this book. Bob's *TARL* approach has changed the way I do business. His ability to break complex methods into understandable action steps makes it easy to jump start your business in the right direction!"

Erica Cosminsky
TheSmallBusinessTranscriptionist.com

"I LOVE this book! As a stay at home dad with 5 kids, I needed a book like Take Action! Revise Later to keep me focused on the simple things in my business so I can spend more time with my family. I felt like Bob was across the table giving me solid advice like he would give any friend or client. Quick to read, easy to apply, these lessons will guide you to success, too."

Chris Morris
TheInternetDad.com

Praise for Bob The Teacher's Coaching

"With Bob's coaching and continued support, I prioritized my projects, plugged them into a time frame and brought my products to market in record time. Following his SIMPLE business plan and adopting his Take Action Revise Later philosophy, I've done more in the last 6 months than the last 2 years! I created and published my first book, created an online training program for authors, increased my income, and expanded the reach of my online radio show, Conversations About Marketing. If you are looking for success online, I have four words for you, "Take Action Revise Later!""

D'vorah Lansky
Author of *Connect, Communicate, and Profit*
TheBlogStation.com

"Bob gave me focus, clarity, and vision—elements I was sorely missing before working with him. Now, instead of spinning many plates, I am moving forward in a logical fashion as I continue to grow my online business. I've launched an internet radio show, streamlined my website, and created an automated communication system that will pay dividends into the future. Most importantly, I get to spend more time with family as a result!"

Meredith Eisenberg
Albuquerque, New Mexico
TameTheInternetMonster.com

"Before coaching with Bob, I was floundering in a mass of ideas, information, and contradictory goals accumulated over too long a period of preparation. I was paralyzed by not even being able to formulate the relevant questions. Knowing that Bob would not settle for less than a successful outcome to our coaching gave me confidence to fully engage in the process, and trust his leadership. And now, my dream of improving the relationships of grandparents around the world with their grandchildren is becoming a profitable reality!"

Ronda Kay Wasser
Jerusalem, Israel
GrandGifting.com

"To put things simply, save yourself 3 years of trial and error and absorb everything you can from Bob Jenkins. His TARL approach has changed the way I do business. With Bob's help and direction, I take my ideas, buckle up and implement them as quickly as possible. As a result of coaching with Bob, I created a coaching program that complements my transcription company, and had my best month ever immediately after I started coaching with him. Bob has a wealth of knowledge and innovative ways to make your business more profitable as he did for mine. I value his advice above all others. Bob's ability to break complex methods into understandable action steps makes it easy to jump start your business in the right direction."

Erica Cosminsky
TheSmallBusinessTranscriptionist.com

"Learning from Bob is like landing in Oz—everything goes from black and white to full color. Thanks to Bob's masterful guidance, my business focus is clearer, more directed and constantly expanding to new levels of awareness. I really get excited about working with the fabulous and energetic Fast Track Master Class members. They are helping to spread my message by opening so many doors (and windows) for me—including in-studio radio and TV interviews that until recently, I could only dream about!"

MaryAnn D'Ambrosio
Newington, Connecticut
LeapWithoutLimits.com

TAKE ACTION!
Revise Later

A Simple Guide to Success in Business

TAKE ACTION!
REVISE LATER

*A Simple Guide
to Success in
Business*

BOB THE TEACHER JENKINS

Skylar
Publications

Leland, NC

Published by Shylar Publications
1114 New Pointe Boulevard, Suite 100-98
Leland, North Carolina 28451
contact@takeactionreviselater.com
TakeActionReviseLater.com

Media Inquiries and Speaking Engagements
For media inquiries, visit
TakeActionReviseLater.com/media
To have Bob speak at your next live or virtual event, visit
TakeActionReviseLater.com/speaker

Limits of Liability and Disclaimer of Warranty
The author and publisher shall not be liable for your misuse of this material. This book is strictly for informational and educational purposes.

Warning—Disclaimer
The purpose of this book is to educate and entertain. The author and/or publisher do not guarantee that anyone following these techniques, suggestions, tips, ideas, or strategies will become successful. The author and/or publisher shall have neither liability nor responsibility to anyone with respect to any loss or damage caused, or alleged to be caused, directly or indirectly by the information contained in this book. Assume the author is remunerated for purchases made from links in this book.

ISBN 13: 978-0-9829851-3-7

Library of Congress Control Number: 2010913602

First Shylar Publications printing: September 2010

Share TAKE ACTION! *Revise Later* with Your Friends, Colleagues, and Community!

I bet you can think of others you know that would benefit from the lessons in this book. Take advantage of the volume discount I'm excited to offer you!

TAKE ACTION! *Revise Later*
A Simple Guide to Success in Business

Single Copies – $17.97 US
5-20 Books – $14.97 each
21-50 Books – $12.97 each
51-100 Books – $9.97 each
101-250 Books – $7.97 each
251+ Books – $6.97 each

To save with your bulk order, visit:
TakeActionReviseLater.com/bulk

WHAT'S INSIDE

Contents

FOREWORD
by Adam Urbanski

This little book offers you three big gifts:

- Mindset shifting stories,

- A step-by-step guide how to turn your passion into a thriving business faster and with greater ease, and

- Inspiration to get the heck out of your own way, stop procrastinating and start succeeding!

Chances are you are exploring reading this book because you want to build a more successful business but something is holding you back. For most people it's these three challenges:

One, you are a technician trying to build a business. It doesn't make you a bad person, but it just has you stuck thinking too small, being busy doing the wrong things and not getting the results you want. *Take Action! Revise Later* will help you understand how to think like an entrepreneur and what you really need to be focusing on to make progress faster.

Two, you don't know what to do next. After all, you didn't go to school to be a business owner and you didn't take any business building classes, right? So this book will be your practical guide, showing you, step-by-step, which specific actions to take next.

And three, you aren't implementing fast enough what you already know. Let's face it, most of us are excellent procrastinators. Our parents and schools have made sure that we "take the time to think about it." This is really where *Take Action! Revise Later* will impact you the most. Giving you practical tools and the inspiration to get going now!

But how can an ex high-school teacher possibly know how to grow a business? That's what I asked myself when I first met Bob. We were speaking at the same conference and when I heard his presentation I instantly realized we have two things in common: we love to teach and we teach in a way that inspires big thinking but simplifies big ideas into immediately usable action steps.

Later, when Bob came to me as a client and shared what he was doing that, in only 18 months, allowed him to retire from his job and make more money than he ever could have dreamt of making as a high school teacher, I immediately asked him, "Why aren't you teaching THIS?" You see, Bob has discovered, used, and perfected a system, that—when followed—will allow anyone to turn their passion, skills, know-how, or hobby into an online business capable of making them wealthy! And he made it simple too!

Fortunately for you, he has taken my advice and has now outlined his simple system in this book. Plus he wrapped it in personal stories and metaphors that will break down your old ways of thinking about business and marketing, instill a new, more effective entrepreneurial mindset, and inspire you to think bigger and act faster.

If you want to make your dream of building a successful business come true, and you are looking for an action guide that will give you step-by-step instructions and the proverbial "kick in the pants" at the same time, this book is for you.

Adam Urbanski
The Millionaire Marketing Mentor® and creator
of the Attract Clients Like Crazy System™
AttractProfitsLikeCrazy.com

INTRODUCTION

*"The mediocre teacher tells.
The good teacher explains.
The superior teacher demonstrates.
The great teacher inspires."*
William Ward

This book is designed to make you think.

- To think about and clarify the mission of your business.
- To think about the impact you want to have in the world and the legacy you wish to leave.
- To think differently about the obstacles that appear to be in your way.

Most importantly, this book is designed to help your business grow because I know the impact your success will have on the rest of the world.

This is a book of lessons, observations, realizations, specific actions, and recommendations. They come from my successes and mistakes. I've written this book to help you to get over those mental blocks that are keeping you from the wild success you deserve.

I opened the Introduction with one of my favorite "teacher quotes." Have you had a teacher who's inspired you at some point in your life, and without whom you would not be where you are today? I hope to be that person for you a year from now, that you'll be in a place you wouldn't have been if it weren't for reading this book.

Living vicariously through the success of my students is something I've long grown accustomed to. So by all means, take these lessons and integrate what you learn into your business and life.

How to Get the Most from this Book

You probably have some goals with this book. Write them down before you get too far.

You'll notice it's comprised of short sections, quotes, and anecdotes to make various points. I've done this deliberately so you can pick it up, do a quick read over a lesson that interests you, and then get back to work.

But to get the most from this book, I suggest you find a comfortable chair in your house or your favorite neighborhood coffee shop and read this cover to cover. Have a pen with you, so you can write in the margins; highlight the ideas that turn on your inner light bulb. Dog-ear your favorite lessons. And take action on the most important ideas that fire you up.

After reading through the book, you should keep it on your desk for easy reference. Pick it up frequently for a dose of motivation, or for a reminder of simple actions you should be focused on to move your business forward.

And at some point, when you feel the book has served its purpose in your life, pass it on to a colleague who could also benefit from these lessons.

I really appreciate that you are reading this book, so I'm going to deliver my best for you.

As you read, I encourage you to share your "eurekas" or "ah-ha" moments with me and others on Twitter.com. Use @BobTheTeacher and the hashtag #TARL so we can all see how you are using these lessons in your business.

You can also post your actions, results, and questions on our growing community on Facebook.

- TakeActionReviseLater.com/fb

Why Are You Here?

Before we begin with the lessons, an important question needs to be asked:

"Why are you here?"

For six years, I started each of my world religions classes with this question. But I'm not asking you to answer this question in a cosmic or religious sense.

I'd simply like you to reflect on why you picked up this book. Why are you in business at this particular moment in time? What are you hoping to achieve over the next three months? The next year? Five years?

Answers to these questions comprise your "Why," and it is a very powerful force. Getting crystal clear on this question is essential to your truly realizing the impact you and your business will have on our planet.

If you *know your why*, you can better understand the path you are traveling down.

If you *write down* your why, and put it in your office, you'll have a "friend" to lean on when times get tough -- and they will!

If you *share your why* with your family, you'll have a stronger support system that will help you overcome any challenge that comes your way.

And if you *put your why into everything you do*, whatever product or service you develop will be true to you. When you engage in an authentic business, you can best serve your customers. That results in great returns and a healthy business.

Don't just say you want more profit. Express specific goals in both dollars and lifestyle changes. What does your next level of success look like for you?

Take a few minutes now, and brainstorm three reasons why you are taking this journey. And be as specific as possible with your why.

Then picture yourself exceeding it, and move forward with that first step!

BobTheTeacher.com

P.S. SHARE YOUR WHY!

Head over to TakeActionReviseLater.com/why and share your why with other readers of this book. Together we can cheer you on toward success!

TAKE ACTION
REVISE LATER

"Most people live and die with their music still unplayed. They never dare to try."

Mary Kay Ash

The world needs what you've got, and we're not going to wait around for you to make sure it's 100 percent ready. In fact, the longer it takes you to bring your gifts to the world, the more likely we'll find what we need from somebody else!

Take action, revise later!

This is my own personal motto, and I encourage you to adopt it as part of your own business philosophy.

You'll find examples throughout the book, but I would like to make sure the concept is crystal clear from the beginning. I'll be sharing lessons from my decade of service in a public high school, as well as from five-plus years building my own successful business from scratch.

The first time you do something, it's likely going to be hard, uncomfortable, and, shall we say, less than stellar. It's the one time you'll likely screw up the most. You may hesitate to move forward out of fear of looking like a fool.

Get over it!

In the classroom, I mentored six student teachers. As I had when I went through the same process, these interns struggled to translate what they had learned in the textbooks into the reality of the classroom.

The scariest day for an intern is that day when they get to be in charge of the class for the first time. Although they wouldn't admit it, each one had a look in their eyes that said, "You know what? I'm still not quite ready." But they had to learn that life doesn't give you the luxury of ever being 100 percent ready. You just have to do.

They were comforted by me giving them permission to be terrible when they started. I told them flat out: "You are going to make mistakes—get over that fact." The trick is to learn from your good days and your bad days, make the adjustments, and become the teacher you want to be.

The same is true for parents with their first child. No matter how many baby books an expectant mother or father reads, nothing quite prepares them for the realities of a newborn in the house.

And of course, I bet you're going through a similar practice in business—no matter what level of experience you already have. The reality of what you're going through now doesn't match the pretty brochure that entrepreneurship promises.

As an internet marketing teacher, I often get asked by my students when they will know that their website is ready to be published online. And they're shocked when I tell them "yesterday." No matter how ugly it is, get it out there, and then revise, revise, revise.

Put your work out there. Get it done, and then adjust according to the data and feedback you get from actual customers.

Inaction dooms a business. But taking action and revising later rewards you.

I actually learned to apply this motto to business in early 2007. I was working on my biggest project to date, an internet marketing course called Squidoo Secrets. I had been using Seth Godin's Squidoo.com platform to attract traffic to my websites and generate leads for my business, without paying a dime in advertising.

My success with Squidoo included having one of my pages (called lenses) appear in the New York Times (April 10, 2006), and appearing at the top of the search engines for excellent keyword phrases—again, without my having spent money to do it.

People who saw my success wanted to know what I was doing, so I decided to create a course about it in the evenings while I was still teaching full-time during the day.

In October and November, I created several video tutorials to show the steps anyone can take to create and optimize "lenses" for their business. My mentor, who introduced me to Squidoo in the first place, interviewed me for the introductory lesson. And I turned that call into an e-book. I did a few additional audio calls with others to have real-life demonstrations of how others could replicate my system.

I then set to work on getting the website ready. November quickly passed by, as did December, then January. February was starting and Squidoo Secrets was still not released, even though it was 90 percent complete. To me, it just wasn't ready yet.

Luckily, I was in a mastermind with a fitness and goal-setting expert, Scott Tousignant (see his program at MindsetSecrets.com, for example).

He asked me why it was taking me so long to release this project, when I knew that so many people could benefit from it. Three months had passed from when I created the core of the course, yet it still wasn't out there. I told him it wasn't ready yet, and I added a few lame excuses that he completely didn't buy (thankfully!).

After his encouragement to set a deadline for only a week later, I launched the site. Within three weeks, that project had generated over $25,000 in revenue. Not bad for a teacher earning about $3,800/month at that point!

More importantly, the feedback I received from the initial customers gave me the exact steps to take to improve the course. I also learned that the customers actually appreciated having their voices heard and seeing the improvements that came about as a result.

Since that time, I've continued to impact other people's lives by creating and delivering over 30 training programs online and in person. They are never perfect! But what I do helps people.

Meanwhile, those that struggle to complete projects under the name of perfectionism wallow in their lack of progress. I don't want that to be you.

The world needs what you have. The status quo is no longer acceptable. Be confident that you've got the goods!

Take action, revise later. We can't wait any longer!

2

CORRECTION TAPE VS. THE DELETE KEY

Are you preprogrammed to avoid mistakes like the plague instead of taking action and revising later?

If so, this could be a function of when you grew up—so it's not your fault if you have trouble adopting the TARL philosophy at first. But it is your responsibility to make that beneficial change for yourself.

At first, what I'm about to teach you could sound like an ageist argument, especially if you are older than forty-five when reading this. Take it to heart, though, and you'll likely find it quite liberating.

The idea is simply this: people who learned certain skills in the age of computers have a bit of an advantage when it comes to the Take-Action-Revise-Later mantra. Fundamentally, the idea is about the inconvenience of mistakes in your communication, and how that may affect the other areas of your life.

An extreme example may help illustrate it even less offensively.

If you grew up in the time of feather pens and inkwells, then you had to be extremely careful when writing a letter.

A single drop of ink spilled onto the page, or a simple misspelling, would result in an entire piece of parchment being ruined—a very costly mistake indeed.

Fast forward to using regular ink pens (before erasable Papermates®), and you'd similarly find mistakes to be a pain. As a student, I remember how annoying it was to be forced to write essays in ink in a timed writing environment in school.

Some teachers were extremely picky about how messy your paper could be, knocking off points if you had scribbled out mistakes or were simply revising your thoughts to make the point clearer. This, of course, discouraged fast thinking and revision, ostensibly in the name of clarity and perfection.

Moving forward in history, there are those who learned how to type with a typewriter—the clickety-clackety ones with the letters that stuck together if you went too fast. Plus, if you made a single mistake on a page, even on the very last sentence of a page you just spent five to ten minutes typing, you'd have to start all over.

Then correction tape—and then Wite-Out®—came along, which allowed you to go over your mistakes without having to start from scratch. It was a vast improvement, much like getting erasers on pens and pencils, but it still left evidence of the mistake.

I was born during Gerald Ford's presidency and had the advantage of learning how to type on a Commodore 64. The age of the personal computer has given us more freedom to take action and revise later.

First, computers came with Delete and Backspace keys to delete and fix the mistakes. Later came the Find/Replace options which made mass corrections possible.

But my favorite development of the computer was when UNDO came along. Now you could realize you made a mistake—no matter what kind—and you could click the UNDO button and all was right again.

Weren't you even more impressed when Multiple-Undo came along, and you could correct not just the last mistake you made, but you could go back five, ten, twenty or more mistakes and fix them in a snap?

So those of us who grew up communicating with this tool in the age of DEL and UNDO have a natural inclination toward taking action and revising later. This communication technology doesn't punish us for making mistakes—a stark contrast to those times when it was both costly and embarrassing to make the same kinds of errors.

Unknowingly, if you learned to write with pen and paper or typewriters, you likely are still impacted by the inconvenience of mistakes.

It's unfortunate that it's impacted you for this long, but now that you know, you can do something about it!

THE OXYGEN MASK THEORY

Have you ever flown on a plane?

Perhaps you can easily recall the preflight routine of flight attendants, describing the safety measures to give you some sense of confidence that all will be well if the plane goes through some sort of trouble.

At some point, you're reminded of what to do in the case of a loss of cabin pressure.

An oxygen mask will drop from the panels above, and you are to place the bright yellow mask over your nose and mouth.

The flight attendants continue, saying that if you are traveling with small children, you should put your mask on first before helping your kid.

When I first heard this as a kid myself (about eight years old), I thought, what about me? Shouldn't my parents help me first to make sure I'm OK?

But as I grew up, I understood better why this made perfect sense.

If parents sacrifice their own breathing to help their kids first, they may not be around to help their children through the next part of the emergency.

Since then, I've implemented this "oxygen mask theory" in different areas of my life.

Basically, we need to take care of ourselves if we are to be as effective at helping other people as we want to be. This isn't about being selfish, but of thinking long-term instead of short-term.

At the basic level, this means taking care of our functional needs before we can be effective for others. And at the advanced level, this means having our best impact by becoming the best we can be.

An example from the classroom may be helpful to make this crystal clear.

Like highly driven business professionals, teachers can burn the candle at both ends for long stretches of time. In an attempt to go all-out to help students, their dedication can actually backfire.

For example, during certain periods of the year, my obligations and responsibilities stacked on top of one another. I so badly wanted to give the students in my school and classroom the best education possible that I took on too many responsibilities. Between the lesson plans, parent-teacher conferences, after-school study sessions, and grading papers, my plate was full enough. But I'd also add coaching the academic team (and later the tennis team), designing ninth-grade team after-school programs and study-skill seminars, teaching other teachers technology, running the school's website, and more.

Although I'm very proud of all I accomplished at the school, I also know that the workload took its toll on the quality of my teaching during occasional periods of exhaustion. I remember teaching a few classes when sleep deprivation and work fatigue was adding up. My lesson plans were so poorly executed, I doubt there was any learning going on—except "how not to teach a class".

I was beyond cranky, and students received curt and unfriendly responses to very simple and genuine questions.

Luckily those were very rare times, because I frequently reminded myself of the Oxygen Mask Theory.

As a business owner, if I don't take time to recharge my batteries, or what Stephen R. Covey calls "sharpening the saw," then my results will eventually be inferior; I'll actually be letting my customers down.

You also need to pay attention to the health of your business before you expend all your energy helping others. If you start out doing a lot of *pro bono* work or volunteering for your community before you've achieved at least some minor level of success, you'll be less effective.

Strike a balance between tithing your time and/or money and growing your business. This will lead to a long-term impact that can truly make a difference on a larger scale.

4

Do You Really Have What it Takes?

Many of us dream of making the big bucks with our own businesses. Are you one of those people?

As my business grew, I discovered a special combination of mindset and skills are needed to become a successful business owner. These skills are, in no particular order:

- Risk taking
- Turning "failures" into rungs up the ladder of success
- Action taking
- Decision making
- Follow through
- Idea generation
- Outsourcing your weaknesses
- Finding what's inside of you that people are willing to pay for
- Turning your best knowledge into products
- Going outside your comfort zone
- Openness to learning new things
- Readiness to learn from experienced mentors

Unfortunately, these are things that not many people are talking about these days. Instead of focusing on the real entrepreneurial skill set you need to be successful, most e-books, mentoring programs, etc., just give you tactics: how to use Pay-Per-Click, how to build a list, how to use affiliate marketing, etc.

Grade yourself on how good you are at each area. And where you find a gap, look to role models and mentors to help you increase your aptitude.

Over time, you'll get better at each one—especially if you dedicate yourself to the improvement.

5

6 Business Lessons Pulled from the HAT

Some of my proudest accomplishments as an educator came as the sponsor and coach of the Hammond Academic Team (HAT) in Columbia, Maryland. We competed on the *It's Academic* TV show (the longest running game show on television) and in local, regional, and national competitions.

During my ten years in that position, we won two state titles. But more importantly, I learned a few important lessons that can easily be applied to business.

Let me share them with you now. I call them the HAT Lessons.

HAT Lesson #1—Make It a Win-Win

When I interviewed for my first teaching job in August 1997, the principal asked me if I would be able to coach a sport (isn't that the first question they ask of all social studies teachers?).

I hadn't developed my tennis skills to the point of coaching, but I had been a trivia nut all my life. So I asked instead if there was an academic team to coach instead.

There was, but it already had a coach.

However, the current coach, a wonderful woman and social studies teacher named Annette Heaps, was to retire within the next two months. Mrs. Heaps was one of those highly respected teachers I wished I could have learned from longer, both as a student and as a new teacher in search of a mentor.

Nevertheless, her retirement at that moment proved beneficial to both of us. She was able to relax, knowing that the team would be in good hands; I inherited a well-trained team of students and got to coach something I loved.

This shows how the best exchanges are a win-win for both parties involved. Each of us came away feeling like we got the better end of the deal.

Mrs. Heaps began her retirement, which I at age 22 put no real value on. And she had already received the value she wanted to from coaching the team.

We each got what we wanted without feeling like we slighted the other.

Are you conducting business this way? Do you put your customers in a winning position, while feeling like you also get great value from the exchange?

*"Someone who needs cash might dig up a DVD
player in the closet and sell it to someone else wanting
to save money by buying a used item."*

Meg Whitman, former CEO and President of eBay

HAT Lesson #2—Get Your Ego Out of the Way

Everybody needs a little dose of humble pie now and then. But as leaders, we can make a bigger difference when we get our egos out of the way.

When I was in high school, our academic team won the Brevard County, Florida, championship, and I competed in the state championships in Disney World.

Then, as a student at the Florida State University, I was part of the FSU College Bowl team. We traveled around the United States competing against other universities.

So when I became the coach at Hammond, I initially walked in with a sense of superiority, and I couldn't wait to show them how smart their new coach was.

That was short-lived for sure!

I helped the team practice by competing with and against them. And it didn't take long for me to realize how much faster and smarter they were than I was.

At first this was intimidating. How could I coach kids to success when they had already surpassed me?

I imagine this is how parents feel when their kids are growing up too, and they bring home those confounded math problems; but not being a parent myself, it was the first time I had this experience.

In business, we often find that new companies come along and do things faster, cheaper, etc.

How are we to compete?

We may hire employees that have mastered skills that we find extremely frustrating. Or they have ideas that we wish we had come up with.

Will they take us seriously as their boss?

As a coach, I recognized that helping these students harness their skills was necessary. They may independently have had great abilities, but they still needed to work together if they wanted to win.

They could also learn from my experiences in competition, and I could study elements of their talent that I could look for in others later (see Lesson #6 below).

In other words, I had to quickly discard thoughts of inferiority and take on a mantle of leadership instead.

Your kids, employees, customers, even your competition aren't looking for you to be better than they are at individual skills. They're looking to you for inspiration and support so they can become better, feel more connected to their purpose, and be rewarded for it.

That first team went on to win the It's Academic Baltimore Championship. And I still thank David, Matt, and Francis for teaching me this important lesson.

HAT Lesson #3—Create Experiences to Build Your Reputation

In addition to being on the television show, the academic team competed against other schools in regional and national tournaments. These typically were hosted at colleges or at other high schools.

After going to many as a student myself, and then again as a coach, I realized that tournaments were quite beneficial to the host school.

Those schools that hosted tournaments tended to have higher reputations in the community, received good press, and generated much-needed revenue for their programs.

Since I wanted to build up Hammond's reputation as well, I decided that we should have our own tournament, too. Plus, I believed it would prove to be an excellent training exercise for our students to write great questions for the event.

Thus, the first annual Green Eggs and Hammond Academic Tournament was born—with apologies to Dr. Seuss. Eventually we ran eight tournaments while I coached the team, and more have been held since I retired from teaching.

Of course, it started with our first tournament, which definitely had its fair share of problems.

For example...

- we started over an hour late, and ended three hours past the anticipated ending time

- our team members were actually writing questions for Round 4 during Round 3 because we fell behind our preparation timeline for the event, and
- a few questions were repeated in later rounds, which caused all sorts of protests among the players and coaches.

Yet, even though the event was far from perfect, the coaches and players had a great time. The real proof came the following year when over 77 percent of the teams returned to GE&H 2; plus another fifteen teams joined them because of word of mouth.

We learned from our mistakes and continued to improve the event so it became one of the most popular academic tournaments.

Using an event to become the center of attention proved quite helpful for our school, too.

One year, an unfortunate incident cast a dim shadow on our school in the eyes of the community. So I invited the media to attend our GE&H tournament to showcase the better side of our school. The news broadcast from that year's event helped put our school back on the map for good, rather than notorious, reasons.

In this time of social media, I take this "bad press is defeated by good press" philosophy very seriously in my business.

And I encourage you to create experiences for your customers where your reputation is built through your actions and not through rumors or isolated incidents that are out of your control.

Through hosting these tournaments, I learned a lot of skills that I later used to grow my business: planning, managing talent, budgeting and cash flow, attracting customers, and using publicity.

HAT Lesson #4—Never Reinvent the Wheel

Running those tournaments and teaching history for ten years also taught me a lot about becoming more efficient.

Teachers may have the summers off, but they work their butts off during the school year. Although the salaries are typically based on a 37-hour week, I often found myself clocking in over 50 hours of grading, planning, filling out paperwork, communicating with students and parents, and attending meetings.

So add to that workload the rigors of running an academic tournament, and you're left with very little time, indeed.

What helped me succeed and not go crazy was remembering not to reinvent the wheel. Instead of starting a lesson plan from scratch, I could lean on my colleagues to give me a foundational plan I could modify.

Then, in following years, I could use the previous lessons and make them even better.

I also learned how to use shortcuts on the computer to reduce the time it took to complete lessons, tests, and handouts. These included the formatting styles in Word, so I spent a lot less time adjusting fonts, spacing, and page margins.

This may seem trivial, but learning how to quickly adjust my documents so they printed on two pages instead of three saved me 33 percent of the time standing at the copier.

We created a number of templates for the tournaments, including room assignments, registration processes, score sheets for the games, and standings spreadsheets that automatically determined playoff seedings.

Compiling over 400 questions for each year's tournament also became more efficient as we developed a routine that could be improved year after year.

These ideas continue to find parallels in business practices several years later.

Once I completed my first live workshop, subsequent training seminars became easier to plan with templates. Each seminar's binder requires revisions of pre-existing handouts, instead of starting with a blank slate.

My team uses an e-book template to format my transcripts quickly and easily instead of starting each one from scratch.

The formatting of this book, for example, was relying on templates and styles in the software.

Are you using templates in your business? Or a scratch every time? Imagine how much more p can be, and how much more free time you can sp business when you stop trying to reinvent the whe

HAT Lesson #5—Buzz on the Prepositions

The Hammond Academic Team continued to be the team to beat throughout the decade of my tenure as coach. We consistently finished in the top nine schools out of eighty-one year after year.

The most common question students, parents, and other teachers would ask me was: How can your team answer those questions so fast?

They frequently called the team members mind-readers because of their ability to buzz in so quickly, seemingly even before the question had actually been asked.

The secret behind our success was something we came to call "buzzing on the prepositions". This may get a bit grammatical for a moment, but the concept is simple.

The most important element of a question is frequently a single word that tends to be the object **of a prepositional phrase**.

We'll skip the sentence diagramming for now, but in that last sentence, the prepositional phrase is "of a prepositional phrase," the preposition is "of," and the object is "phrase."

So when a question is asked like, "Who was the first president of the Confederacy?" the word that matters is "Confederacy."

So I coached students to learn how to buzz on the prepositions, and trust that they would know the answer when they heard that key word.

With the speed of natural speech, the person reading the question would say the preposition and the remainder of the phrase before they'd stop when they heard the buzzer.

dents would then get the key word and be able to use their
e seconds to mentally run through their brain and retrieve the
answer to the question.

In the example above, the students would buzz when they heard "of",
knowing that the reader could not stop themselves before saying
"Confederacy."

This is a perfect Take Action Revise Later example because buzzing on
the preposition requires a certain level of confidence to take the risk.
They had to believe that when they heard that word, they would be
able to pull the answer off their mental shelf, and do so quickly.

Knowing that they'd get the question right 80 to 90 percent of the time,
they were able to beat any team that didn't have similar confidence.

In business, we often have to make decisions without all the information presented to us. We have to buzz in when we feel we have
enough information, even though we know we take the risk of not
making the right decision.

If we can act quickly, and be right *most* of the time, then our success
against competition is very likely.

Buzzing on the preposition also relied on a significant development of
knowledge through study, practice, and experience. You have to learn
from the mistakes you do make so you can have the right answer the
next time. Without that, the confidence won't be there.

The first time you hire someone, or work with a particular vendor, or
plan a project, you have to go with what you know much earlier than
when it's totally comfortable. Because if you wait until you're 100 percent certain, you've likely lost your competitive edge.

The best employees get snatched up by somebody else; the vendors
increase their prices; and your new project gets implemented by your
competitors first.

As I coached my students to realize, the probability of you making the
wrong decision decreases the more you develop this particular skill.

HAT Lesson #6—Attract and Manage Your Talent

To run a successful academic team year after year, I had to make sure to attract the best students early and often.

Winning the championship the first year, and continuing to do well on the television show made it easier.

But I also had to foster an environment that was both challenging and enjoyable to the students. Winning isn't the only reason students wanted to join the team—they wanted a place where their unique skills would be both developed and appreciated.

But not all students who wanted to compete were a good fit. Talent alone doesn't make you a great player, especially in a team game.

So I learned over the years that it wasn't enough to bring a bunch of smart kids together and expect magic to happen. Managing the talent was needed to elevate their level of success.

It was customary for the smartest kid on the team to be captain—the captains are the ones that are ultimately responsible for answering the question after listening to the team.

But sometimes the smartest kid didn't listen to the other members and gave wrong answers despite the right one coming from their teammate.

As the coach, I had to learn how to identify what characteristics made the best captain. Sure, they had to know a lot, but they also needed a lot more.

They had to

- be able to listen to both me and to their team members,
- have confidence in both themselves and their teammates,
- be gracious and appreciate their team members, and
- leave their egos behind.

And as their coach, if they didn't have those skills, I had to take the responsibility of picking the person that did—even at the risk of alienating those that felt they "deserved" to be the hotshot of the team.

Coaching this team also showed me the various types of leadership that can surface. And that no one style is the best.

As you grow your business, you've got to attract talent by making sure yours is the company people want to work for.

Do they know they'll be listened to and appreciated? Do they feel that their skills will be used and expanded—and then rewarded appropriately?

Will you pick the right people to help you lead, based on factors beyond convenience or seniority?

And will you be willing to shake things up if you put the wrong pieces together?

Talent alone won't grow your company. It takes a combination of leadership, skills, communication, and correcting as you go.

6

IDENTIFY YOUR DESTINATION

A drive to the Florida Keys for a vacation in Islamorada provided an important lesson on goal setting.

From North Carolina, we took sixteen hours of total travel time to get there. We arrived at night, but in the morning we awoke to breathtaking views of palm trees, crystal blue water, and sunshine.

For the week prior to the trip, we argued a bit about which car to drive there.

Should we take our 2001 Volvo S60 which, at over 76,000 miles, needed a tune-up—but has amazingly comfortable seats?

Or should we rent a Prius and save a lot of money on gas, but perhaps be too cramped for the three of us and our luggage?

Or should we rent a compact SUV that would better fit all of our crap that we were taking, but not be quite as comfortable as our own car, nor as fuel-efficient as the Prius?

Since I had traveled to Chicago the weekend before to speak at an internet marketing conference and ran out of time to take the car for its tune-up, option 1 was eliminated.

Ultimately we decided to go with a Toyota Rav 4 instead of the Prius because of the storage issue. But as we were driving I had one of those moments of clarity…

The vacation was about enjoying three days in the Keys—not about which car to drive to get there.

I was reminded of this distinction when a gentleman called me up to ask for a refund of a product of mine.

Since my refund rate is less than 2 percent, I tend to ask questions to make sure I understand where the problem is and if there was a miscommunication that could have been avoided or can be fixed in the future.

What I learned from this gentleman is typical of the other refund requests that I get. He was too worried about what car he was driving and not focusing enough on the destination.

You see, all of my products are excellent (I know I'm biased, but you know it's true or you wouldn't be reading this book), but they are not perfect solutions for everyone at the same time.

For example, my Teleseminar Formula course is an excellent training program, but if you are trying to master PPC (pay-per-click) marketing or search engine optimization (SEO), it will be distracting to you.

So you may buy Teleseminar Formula because my sales letter is good, and then never look at it because you are really working on something completely different. You look two weeks later at your receipts and decide to ask for a refund, and you may even blame me for my product not solving your Web site problem.

So what does this have to do with which car to rent on a road trip?

Well, we often get caught up in the program, tool, or gizmo, thinking the next shiny thing will be the solution to our problems. A few weeks later, or even a few years later, the program/tool/gizmo chasers are still in the same place they were at the beginning (you probably know this all too well).

If we hadn't decided on a particular car, we would have never enjoyed the palm trees, tropical breezes, and relaxation of the Keys. Even though it was uncomfortable getting there, and cost more than we planned, the vacation itself more than made up for what truly amounts to trivial matters in the big picture.

So, instead of trying to figure out whether one of my courses is the greatest thing since sliced bread, or some guru's traffimagnetronificator will make you a gazillion dollars...

... step away from the gizmos, and look instead at the destination you are trying to reach.

What I hope you'll realize is that it's not the car you drive, but where you're headed that counts the most. Get that clear in your mind first, and any good program you do invest in will help you get there with more certainty.

7

DEFEATING PARALYSIS BY ANALYSIS WITH THE GOLDEN TRIAD

If you are at the starting point of your business, you may feel overwhelmed with all the things you need to do to get going. You may receive so much information from so many different sources that you get confused and end up doing nothing.

Confusion and analysis paralysis are common issues for people at the starting gate.

Here are a few points to help you get off the launch pad.

First: be patient. It took me months to really get anything going, and about a year before I was able to replace my regular job income. It also took specific action and mentoring with experts so I could get help on a regular basis, especially when it came to staying focused.

And think about this. In the offline world, it typically takes up to five years before a business owner is able to turn a consistent profit—and most people that start don't even last past the first three years.

As for where to start with your business, you need to consider what it is that you do well, and how that can be converted into a product or service.

I call this the Golden Triad—mix your passions, your skills, and what the market wants in order to find the sweet spot of your potential success.

What do you love to do, and would do even if you didn't get paid? That's what you're passionate about.

What have you learned through job and life experience that seems to come second nature to you? Also think about what people come to you for, because you seem to do it so easily. These are your skills.

To find what the market wants, you need to ask questions. Use Twitter, your customer list, neighbors, and community leaders what they want in the areas of your skills and passions. Check online forums for active threads around key issues your market actively discusses.

You should be able to find that specific idea that you can do easily, love to do, and that people will pay you for.

All other opportunities and information you receive that do not help you take your Golden Triad to market should be discarded.

8

SOS—SHINY OBJECT SYNDROME

Do you get distracted easily by opportunities?

You may be suffering from Shiny Object Syndrome (SOS).

To battle SOS, you must first realize you have a limited amount of time in the day. Focus your energy on e-mail during specific times of the day, get as much done during a defined period of time, and turn it off. This helps you ignore a lot of the opportunities and distractions when you are trying to be most productive.

How to Pick What to Buy

Just like you, I'm still likely to get distracted by shiny things, want to find additional ways to grow my business, etc. But I've learned something about what I've bought in the past.

If I invest in too many things at the same time, no matter how great each one is individually, ALL of them fail to produce results.

It's only when I buy one thing and apply it with complete focus for a few weeks or months, that I get real results from any particular product.

With all the barrage of buying opportunities, it's difficult not to see the value in each software product, e-book, home-study course, or seminar series. And the temptation is that each one can explode your business.

The reality is, buying them all will implode your business, no matter how good they are individually. Frustration results and more debt accumulates for no good reason.

So, what's a business owner who loves learning and fast growth supposed to do?

Ask yourself these questions constantly before you make another investment:

1. What was the last product I purchased?
2. What have I done to implement it?
3. Have I used it to its full potential?
4. Am I ready for another product or service in order to move forward?

If any part of your answer is too many, not enough, not quite, or probably not, then clearly you shouldn't buy the new gizmo.

Trust me: this is very difficult to do consistently. You may trust the people behind the new product based on previous experience or the recommendation of a trusted associate. You may know the quality of work they are putting out there.

But buying great products won't transform your business.

It's taking action on what the products can teach you or do for you that makes the difference.

So whenever you see some new product or marketing service come out, ask yourself those questions above. And before you plunk down another $50, $250, or $5,050 (or more!), carefully decide which ONE product (if any) would be best suited for where you are right now and where you want to go.

Invest in it, shut off all the other offers, and beat that product to death putting it to work for you.

Choose What to Recommend to Your Customers Wisely

If you are in a position of authority in your audience, you can do well to help them avoid SOS, too. Serve as a filter for them, and be selective of what you promote.

When evaluating products to promote, I take a look at several things.

First, I try to evaluate the product itself if it is available. I take a look at the common questions that I get from clients and subscribers from my blog and in my courses and think how the product will address their needs. This eliminates most products that I could recommend.

Second, I look to see what the likelihood is of the product actually being easy to implement (or worth the effort and price) for the majority of people I'm teaching. Sometimes this means I may miss the minority, unfortunately. But I also can tell that if it won't work for me, it's not something I can share with credibility.

Third, I reflect on how respectfully the product owner treats his or her customers. Will they be barraged with useless e-mails after buying? Or will they be taken care of?

And follow up with your current customers about their results with your recommendations. If a majority doesn't find them useful, then maybe you should revise which suggestions you make to new customers later.

9

ARE YOU BUILDING A BUSINESS OR CHASING MONEY?

There is a fundamental difference between trying to make money and building a business.

Making money is an activity where you chase sales. When your goal is focused on money alone, everybody knows it. Hence nobody buys because it seems like the end result is just going to benefit you and not them.

Building a business is where you build relationships, solve specific problems your customers are facing, and do so in a way that you can do really well. You then offer the same customers additional ways to help them over time.

I call it Helping People Profitably.

The only real way I know of to build a business around relationships is to have a clear understanding of what skills and passions you can combine to address the needs of your market. The solutions you provide must be obviously connected to your abilities and background or else your potential customers will think you are just trying to sell them something.

10

MONUMENTAL METAPHORS

During a trip to speak at an internet marketing conference in Washington, D.C., I had several "ah-has." They came to me as I played tourist—walking to the standard spots around the Federal Triangle.

You just never know when you'll be inspired, especially if you are a former history teacher. The following are what I call "Monumental Metaphors," and I imagine that you'll never look at famous landmarks the same way again. For video versions of these metaphors filmed on location, head over to:

- TakeActionReviseLater.com/mms

At the Lincoln Memorial: Be Presidential

When you run your own business, especially from home, you often find yourself doing a lion's share of the work.

But are you spending more of your time as the president, or as the groundskeeper?

Like most presidents, Abraham Lincoln delegated many of the every-day tasks of his administration to his Cabinet members and other officials.

Can you imagine Lincoln trying to do everything to run the country in the middle of the Civil War without getting help from specialists? You would never expect him to research all the details of monetary policy, transcontinental railroad land acquisition, overseas negotiations, troop movements throughout the Union, and all the laws that Congress was trying to pass—right?

Instead, he had to surround himself with advisors he could trust to help him filter that information so he can make the best decisions he could.

No one would ever claim Lincoln to be an infallible president, either. Yet he remains one of history's best, because he didn't try to do everything himself.

So why are you trying to keep up with all the latest technologies, techniques, business models, and customer trends by yourself?

Surround yourself with trustful advisors.

If you're like me, and you're working from home with no employees, that may mean to pick a few "distant" mentors who you listen to through e-mail or coaching calls.

You may also want to select one or two virtual employees who take care of administrative tasks so you can focus on the larger picture.

And you should also give yourself permission to push 90 percent of what you're being distracted by to the back burner, so that the remaining 10 percent can actually accelerate your business.

At the White House: Strike a Life/Work Balance at Your Home Office

Perhaps the most famous home office in the world is the White House. The 2008 election brought Barack Obama into residence, along with his wife and two daughters.

Early in his presidency, Obama has articulated a clear priority of balancing his family time with his work-at-home life. Regardless of your views on his politics, this balancing act is important to learn from if you are a home-office business owner.

Like Obama, and the forty-three presidents before him, you should have a distinct area of your home for business. Ideally it should be separated from distractions like where the kids play, the television, the kitchen, etc. Productivity is one thing that can suffer from having a home office that's too much "home" and not enough "office."

You also need to set time boundaries that you expect your family to honor, but that you also respect. Work time is "do not disturb" time, except for emergencies. But on the flip side, when you say you'll be finished for the day, stick to that schedule as much as possible.

The just-a-minutes and be-there-in-a-secs are no substitute for sticking to your promises of family time. Occasionally, sacrifices need to be made, of course—especially during the start up phase. But the support of your family that will fuel your long-term growth may be what you're sacrificing, instead, if you don't strike a good balance.

At the Washington Monument: Finish What You Start

You may have noticed that the monument dedicated to the first President of the United States has two distinct shades of marble. This is because the initial construction was halted for a couple of decades because of a lack of funding. It wasn't finished until thirty-six years after the first stone was set.

You should have "big ideas" in your business. But make sure that you can actually finish them, or the benefits to your customers will never materialize.

Improperly implemented, the Take Action Revise Later philosophy can result in a number of unfinished projects. This is especially true if your budget process is overly ambitious, like it was for the Washington Monument.

The original plan for it also included a colonnade and statue of George Washington. But those that finished the project knew that it was *good enough* to open to the public, instead of waiting to spend even more money making it perfect.

What project of yours is still waiting to be perfect before you release it?

At the Reflecting Pool: Take Time to Evaluate Your Goals and Your Progress Toward Them

Between the Lincoln Memorial and the Washington Monument is the Reflecting Pool. On a still day, with the sun shining, it's a beautiful site (unless you get really close and see what's in the water).

It serves as a mirror to emphasize the majesty of the monument. But it also serves as a point of reflection for us, too.

The essence of Take Action Revise Later is that you *do* now, but you frequently evaluate the results to continue to do better. Unfortunately, most people don't take the time to evaluate what those results are. They continue to do the same thing, without altering course based on the evidence in front of them.

Reflecting time should be scheduled into your week, like a meeting with your most important client. At the end of the week, take stock on what you accomplished—and celebrate it! Look back to the goals you had set for your business this week, and see how well you met, exceeded, or fell short of them.

Evaluate the data—both anecdotal and measurable. And be honest with yourself about what worked and what didn't. Adjust accordingly, and repeat the process every week.

Spend a few minutes each day in a mini-reflection period, too. This not only helps you keep on track better, it can also help you be realistic about budgeting your time and money so you don't overburden yourself or your team.

And of course, quarterly and annual reflections of the "big picture" can be of tremendous help to the long-term health of both you and your business.

At the Thomas Jefferson Memorial: Don't Let Your Principles Suffer Because of Your Finances

It's not a secret that Thomas Jefferson had slaves while professing his disdain for the practice. This hypocrisy has its roots in Jefferson's poor financial state.

According to Jefferson, he wanted to free his slaves during his lifetime, but couldn't because of the large debt with which he was burdened. While this can be considered true, or a convenient excuse, the point is still valid for us to learn from.

Your principles should not be sacrificed because of bad financial decisions that affect your business. Ultimately, you have to look at yourself in the mirror each day. Cutting corners at the expense of your customers, or getting into uncomfortable situations in an attempt to get out of debt, will hinder your success.

This is another example of the Oxygen Mask Theory at work, of course. Without staying true to your beliefs and principles while also ensuring financial stability, you'll have a difficult time fulfilling the purpose of your business.

Even worse for your business, your customers will leave you if they sense hypocrisy in your marketing or fulfillment of your products.

At the US Capitol Building: Run Your Ideas Past Other People

It may seem odd for me to use the official houses of the US Congress as a lesson in Take Action Revise Later. After all, it can notoriously take months to pass a bill among all the arguments, motions, amendments, and filibusters there.

However, the essence of having two Houses is useful on many points.

First, you should bounce your ideas off of someone else before you set everything in stone. TARL doesn't mean conducting your business in a vacuum. It means revising as you go based on new information growing out of initial (and subsequent) results from previous actions.

You may not be a C-SPAN junkie like me, but perhaps you've seen a Congressional hearing or a floor debate. One of my favorite lines they say is, "I reserve the right to extend and revise my remarks." You need to give permission to yourself to do the same.

You'll make statements, write blog posts, submit press releases, write books, hold teleseminars, etc.—but even all those don't have to be the last time you speak on that specific topic. Take some of the pressure off of making those things perfect the first time you do them.

Remember that all financial bills must originate in the House of Representatives. If your family is heavily dependent on your business succeeding, and therefore the support of your spouse, kids, and/or siblings, then let your "House" have a stake in the financial decisions of your company (or at least keep them informed).

Congress also takes recesses at least four times per year, even though there's a lot of work left to be done. Make sure you take a break from your business to reenergize your commitment to progress while enjoying the fruits of your labor.

To be reelected, members of Congress have to do what their most influential constituents want—not just what the Congressperson feels they "need". Results matter much more than intent, and if they mess up, their constituents let them know by voting them out of office. In business, you have to stay in touch with your customers, pay attention to what they want—especially the most influential ones. Otherwise, they'll vote with their feet and buy from your competitors.

At the US Treasury: Keep an Eye on Both Income and Expenses

Most businesses fail.

And the biggest reason they fail is because they run out of money. You have to keep an eye on where your money is coming from and account for the spending.

The basic formula for success in business is to spend less than you bring in. Profit is the only way a business can sustain itself over time.

But don't be afraid of leveraging debt to grow your business. Done strategically, you can use outside capital to fund a growth period. Just make sure the risk you take from this burden is outweighed by the resulting growth.

You should also turn to experts to help you with your accounting and bookkeeping. You may think that financial tracking and tax preparation software seems like a money-saver. But the ongoing support of a bookkeeper and the occasional analysis of a CPA can save you a lot of money in wasted expenses. You'll also spend a lot less time trying to keep up with changes in tax laws, and what expenses you can deduct. These professionals can also help you realize what your cash cows are, and which revenue streams are becoming dried-up creek beds.

And here's a bonus tip from the life of Alexander Hamilton, the first Secretary of the Treasury: don't let an argument with a competitor reach the point of becoming a duel.

At the Vietnam Veterans Memorial: Let Your Mess Be a Message

The Vietnam War remains one of the most controversial periods of history. It's a mix of good intent and heroism with tragedy and failure.

The Vietnam Veterans Memorial was designed by Yale graduate student Maya Lin. It serves as a tribute to those Americans who lost their lives, as well as a way to remember the mistakes that were made. Unlike most of the monuments in D.C., its primary purpose is not to celebrate but to illuminate.

Most times, tragedies are swept under the rug, hidden from the view of those that come after. But so much can be learned from mistakes — both our own and those of others.

In an attempt to be professional, we often hide our mistakes from our customers, team members, and coworkers. We think that showing our blemishes will reveal weakness.

But our mistakes should be used as instructions so others can avoid having to learn the hard way.

People also want to know your story — warts and all — so that they can better relate to you and your company. This is especially true if you are a mentor or coach to others.

Your path to success was likely not paved in gold, but in cracked bricks and mud puddles. Turn your mess into your message, and you'll attract better customers and more loyal team members.

11
PROFIT FROM ORGANIZATION THAT WORKS FOR YOU

Are you in control of your business, or does it seem the other way around?

When you are in control, you determine what hours you will work, the time frame for your product launches, and even their growth trajectory.

But when your business is out of control, you are back in the employee role again and have to react to situations as they come up.

What do you do to maintain control of your business, to keep yourself in the driver's seat?

- Do you set goals and check up on yourself periodically?
- Do you set benchmarks and prioritize the stages of your business development?
- Do you have a legal pad by your computer that you use to write your to-do list and weekly targets?

Personally, I have found that if I am organized, and plan strategically and often, my profit increases. When I fail to do that I'm all out of whack.

I've tried all kinds of ways to be organized. I made business cards that were mini-task items that I could shuffle around. I've used day calendars, and desk calendars. I have an idea book with a page or two for each project.

Each one of those systems works for a few days, and then I find myself off track again. In addition, now I have all these pieces of paper lying around my desk piling up without any real sense of organization. Ironic, isn't it?

Fortunately, I've been using a different type of system that I started using in the classroom. It took me a while to apply it to my business. But since doing so, I've been impressed that it has stood the test of time.

The technique I use is mindmapping with free software called Freemind. I'll tell you more about it in a moment, but whatever system you use, stick to it if it works. If it doesn't, be willing to try something new.

12

TURN YOUR TO-DO LISTS INTO MALLEABLE MIND MAPS

Every productivity expert will give you their opinion about how to get more things done in the same amount of time.

They'll show you how to make to-do lists, categorize them with 1, 2, 3, or A, B, C and try to get you to eliminate tasks off your list.

These methods can be helpful for some, but if it's not working for you take a look at mind maps.

Mind maps are simply visual representations of ideas. You've probably used them before to organize your thoughts on a business project, or back in school when you were thinking about writing a paper.

There are plenty of mind-mapping software programs out there, from free to expensive. All have their own merits, but my favorite one to use is Freemind.

This won the medal for me because it's simple, uses a hierarchical structure, and exports maps as images, PDFs, and text outlines.

Let me give you an example of my to-do list from a typical weekend.

- Mow the lawn
- Write an e-mail to subscribers and clients
- Twitter a bit
- E-mail
- Work on sales page for Discover Freemind

- Create survey for IM Success Workshop
- Send inner circle members note about Sunday night call
- Watch Orioles game (somebody has to!)
- Straighten office
- Friend requests on Facebook
- Check fantasy baseball roster
- Post lesson on Freemind to blog

Now if I were writing this on a piece of paper as they come to me, this is the order they would come out.

Traditionally, I would then either rewrite my list, or designate each task as a 1, 2, or 3.

But with Freemind, I can actually move these things around based on categories I determine.

So for example, a regular to-do list map would look like this:

Mow the lawn

write an email to subscribers/clients

Twitter a bit

check email

Work on sales page for Discover Freemind

Create survey for IM Success Workshop

Saturday To Do List

Send inner circle members note about Sunday call

Watch Olympics

straighten office

friend requests on Facebook

Check fantasy baseball roster

Post lesson on Freemind to blog

And I would then set up categories of Home, Office, Just for Fun, and put each task into a category.

Alternatively, I could use things like morning, afternoon, evening.

Just this step alone of categorizing and shifting tasks into slots helps me tremendously. And if I make subcategories to group things by similar processes (i.e., social networking, online/offline work, etc.), I can make sure I am efficient, too.

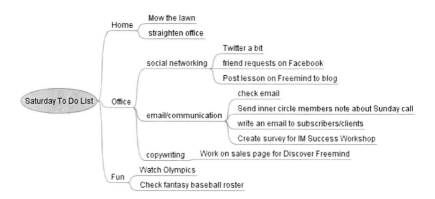

Another cool feature within Freemind is when I'm focusing on a task, I can make the other tasks "disappear" so I am not distracted. That little circle next to a category means they're still there, just tucked away.

I use this same process whether it's a daily agenda, a workshop, a product launch, or a teleseminar—anything that benefits from strategic planning is a perfect fit for mind maps.

One final tip—color helps me in my organization. So I will often use Freemind's formatting tools to help my brain make sense of the map even more. So the map above turns into this:

Typically, I find that using mind maps this way helps me save up to an hour every day in added productivity.

Use mind maps for yourself, but show it to teachers and students you know, too; it's a lifesaver for lesson planning, organizing homework with extracurricular activities, or even developing long-range plans for college!

To download Freemind software free, go to:

- TakeActionReviseLater.com/freemind

13

ARE YOU BRANDED?

Do people remember your name?

In this day and age, it's important that you throw away any conceptions you may have of hiding any ego. Being humble is important, of course. But making sure people know your name and your credentials is crucial in business.

Let me share with you a quick story.

A few years back, I was on a membership forum at WAHM.com, trying to earn the trust of the work-at-home mom community.

As a guy, I was worried that they would see me as someone who was just trying to spam the boards and then leave. So I had to figure out a way to earn their trust.

To do this, I provided value in my posts and didn't spend all my time pitching things to them. I provided helpful answers to members' questions instead of sales pitches.

However, I also wanted to make sure that I stood out by getting them to remember my name. At the same time, I was trying to figure out what my website domain would be, for my home base. And unfortunately, BobJenkins.com was already taken by a successful real estate agent in California.

So while driving home after a long day in the classroom, I came up with Bob The Teacher.

I started using it first on the WAHM boards, and it stuck. I started noticing that people would refer to my posts and comments, AND they would include my name.

That was great publicity—and it didn't cost me a dime.

Then I registered that domain, bobtheteacher.com.

This was back when I was trying to build up a network marketing business. At my first convention with this company, nobody knew who I was when I introduced myself as Bob Jenkins. But when I mentioned my screen name was BobTheTeacher, they instantly recognized me as if I were a celebrity.

And, really, I wasn't. In fact, they were doing better in the business than I was. Nevertheless, because of the attention I received from the leaders, others in the audience credentialed me as an authority, too.

Of course, being a leader is a mindset—we don't need to get into that here.

But the point is, if I hadn't branded myself, and used my name and picture on those message boards, people would never have remembered who I am.

And in this business, name recognition is critical.

So I encourage you to do two things.

First, for any message board or social networking site you ever go on, register your own name, or a very easy to remember nickname. MomInTexas214 just isn't going to cut it.

Then, go register your own domain name, hopefully exactly the same name.

Even if you don't do anything with the domain yet, it reserves a permanent place for you on the internet.

With this domain name, you'll also be able to use a professional e-mail address (see Chapter 20).

Brand yourself, and watch how much faster people start looking to you for advice.

To learn how to register your own domain name, visit:

- TakeActionReviseLater.com/domains

14

6 KEYS FOR A SIMPLE BUSINESS

Being a former high school teacher, I'm a big fan of acronyms. So when I created my flagship training program, I decided to call it SIMPLE—School for Information Marketing Profits—Live Event.

However, SIMPLE stands for a lot more than just an event. In fact, it's a set of elements that guide how a business can be run.

If you believe, like I do, in helping people profitably, and you want to succeed based on your brainpower instead of gimmicks or fads, you should consider a SIMPLE business.

You'll know you're following this model if your business is based on these 6 elements:

- Specialization
- Intelligence
- Monetization
- Portability
- Leverage
- Experiences

Let me explain a bit more about each one.

Is It Specialized?

A primary reason businesses fail to get customers is a lack of specialization. When I first started my business, I was all over the map!

Even my teacher friends asked me, "What are you selling this week, Bob?" Without a clear direction, I couldn't build up trust in the marketplace. And because I wasn't focused on one thing, I never practiced the patience I needed to see things through to profit.

Make sure your customers know *the thing* that you are great at. You don't have to be the best when you start—but it should be clear that what you do is the best thing you should be doing.

What if you're a Renaissance entrepreneur? There's nothing wrong with offering a variety of services to the marketplace. But to the individual buyer checking out your sales page, listening to your teleseminar, or meeting you at an event, make sure one specialty is on the table.

Is It Intelligent?

With such a crowded marketplace, you have to give your customers something your competition cannot: your intelligence. When your brain is central to your business, you make it very difficult to be ripped off.

Turn what you know into a business that actually helps people. Once you start marketing based on your own brainpower and expertise, you will see much better results.

This is the power of information marketing, consulting, and coaching. You'll discover a faster rise to authority because you aren't afraid to stand on your knowledge, experience, and passions.

Is It Monetized?

Do you know the #1 reason why businesses fail?

They run out of money.

So your business has to be monetized, or else you can't last! If people aren't willing to buy what you're selling, always expecting it to be free, then you won't be able to survive your first year in business.

Sure, giving away some of your products for free is a great way to build rapport and attract more potential customers. I've certainly done well with this model. But that's because I've always referred free customers to relevant and high-quality products as an affiliate; and I've always offered premium products or services soon after they receive something free.

Don't be afraid to ask for the sale. Then make sure you return to existing customers and provide them with additional products and services.

Is It _P_ortable?

Some entrepreneurs are perfectly content serving a narrow geographic market or working from an office.

But what happens when external factors interfere?

Having a business that's portable is critical if you wish to enjoy more freedom than you would have with a job. With a portable business, anywhere you can connect to the Internet, you can operate. Since understanding this principle, I've been able to "work" on cruise ships, in foreign countries, around the United States, and even at the neighborhood coffee shop.

Also, if you or your partner or spouse wants to relocate (called by promotion, grandchildren, island living, presidential appointment, etc.), you won't be restricted to customer-based geography. And if oil spills, hurricanes, or other disasters strike, you won't be prematurely shut down.

Is It _L_everaged?

Most entrepreneurs escape the wage-earning life of a soul-sucking day job only to replace it with a time-for-dollars trap in their own business. So you need to focus on creating leverage in your business. This means a few different things.

First, a leveraged business allows you to get paid repeatedly for work you do once. So instead of trading time for dollars, you are earning dollars for products. For example, instead of being paid to speak to an audience once, you might give your talk on a teleseminar that can be replayed by anyone anywhere at any time from your website.

Second, you'll have a leveraged business if you can borrow attention and credibility from others in your field or in compatible industries. Instead of doing all the promotional work yourself, you'll have referrals coming in from your partners.

And third, you can form joint-venture relationships where you and others actually combine forces to serve your market with products and services.

Is It Experiential?

Like you, I receive endless e-mails on a daily basis that promise a four-hour work week, autopilot income, set-and-forget profit machines—you name it. And while in theory those sound great, they really seem kind of boring to me.

Don't get me wrong—I love vacations as much as you do (I spent about thirteen weeks on vacation in the past year)—but like you, I also enjoy working hard and helping people.

So it's important that your business is fun to do. The more experiential you make your business for your customers, the more they enjoy what you do for them.

Don't just create products that are essentially one-way streets. Incorporate interactive products and services to truly connect with your audience. These may be live workshops, teleseminars and webinars, or membership sites where members can participate in forums or within comment zones.

You have plenty of choices for how to run your business. I hope this SIMPLE framework fits the way you think about the ideal business environment!

If you'd truly like to succeed with your own information-based business, learn more about my SIMPLE Training programs, where I teach you how to turn this theoretical structure into a practical, profitable business. Go to:

- TakeActionReviseLater.com/simple

15

CONNECT, CREATE, AND COLLABORATE YOUR WAY TO SUCCESS

Here's a very practical process you can take your business through for accelerated growth.

I call it the Connect-Create-Collaborate model, and it's the cornerstone of my own success in business. Most people try to do these steps in the wrong order, and struggle with frustrating results. If you have the 6 elements of a SIMPLE business in mind, this three-phase path is sure to lead you to success.

Phase 1: Connect People to Solutions

Since you know your industry better than the average customer in that marketplace, you are in a great position to help people locate existing solutions to their problems. You most likely use those resources, tools, and experts yourself—or you did at one point to help you get to where you are now.

Listen to the crowds of potential customers and what they're griping about. Help them to solve those problems by connecting them to the solutions. This could mean you share a software tool that addresses the issue, or you bring their attention to a leading expert's training program that's already up and running.

You can also serve as a filter by reviewing books or courses that help audiences take action and implement those solutions.

During this phase, you'll likely be able to generate revenue as an affiliate of those products and services. And regardless of the income, by serving the marketplace, you'll gain credibility and social capital that will prove beneficial in stages 2 and 3 of this model.

Phase 2: Create the Missing Solutions to Fill the Gaps in Your Marketplace

Whether your Phase 1 takes a few days, or a few months, you'll come away with an added benefit: market research to discover what people are buying and what they're still hungry for. Once you've identified what's missing, you can then create your own products and services to fill in those gaps.

The trouble most entrepreneurs run into is they try this step first. Then they struggle to stand out within a crowded marketplace.

By filling in the gaps, you can serve a niche of your field profitably. And since you already built up a relationship with your audience in Phase 1, you have an eager market that has already told you what they want!

The missing piece you create could deal more specifically to solve additional problems that go unnoticed by the others in your field. Or perhaps you deliver your services and products in ways that the others haven't considered. For example, your audience may want more individual attention than the gurus in your field are willing to offer.

During this phase, you'll generate revenue from selling your own products and services, while continuing to earn revenue recommending the Phase 1 solutions you had already identified.

Phase 3: Collaborate with Customers and Competitors for Faster Growth

Once you have your own products and services, you gain status in your field as a solution provider. And this allows you to sit at the "big table" in your industry.

You'll now be able to partner with others as they help you grow your business with referrals and collaborative projects.

An important step in this process is to connect your products and services to affiliate management software. This provides an incentive to your partners to promote you with the reward of sharing in the revenue (i.e., a commission). If you don't have such a system in place, you can always swap marketing promotions. But using an affiliate program makes the process fair.

You'll be able to turn your customers into affiliate partners, too. As each additional customer enjoys your products and services, doorways to their circle of influence become open to you, as well.

And you'll start hearing yes more often from those in your field for joint projects and promotions. No longer will you be the best-kept secret in your field, but the go-to expert you deserve to be.

Repeat All 3 Phases for Exponential Growth

Perhaps the best part of these three phases is you can repeat the process for continuous growth. In fact, I've used this system over a dozen times over the last few years to become the leading teacher of internet marketing strategies for do-it-yourself entrepreneurs. I know your success is inevitable if you follow this path, as well.

5 Skills to Master for Internet Marketing Profits

If you're going to grow your business with internet marketing, you'll need to master five skill sets. These are especially important for you to learn within the SIMPLE framework and the Connect-Create-Collaborate model I've shared in the last two chapters.

They are:

- Productivity and Time Management
- Relationship Marketing through E-mail and Social Media
- Website Basics
- Creating and Selling Information Products
- Affiliate Management

#1: Productivity and Time Management

Some blame the economy for their poor results, but I would bet that most people aren't growing their businesses due to a lack of focus. You need to have a system in place that keeps you on track and makes the most out of your time.

Personally, I prefer to use mind maps to help set and stay focused on specific goals within my daily, weekly, monthly, and annual time frames. Much more powerful than to-do lists, mind maps allow you to categorize and prioritize those activities that simply must be done to move forward.

Whatever system you use, if you end your day feeling like you accomplished nothing, then that system isn't working for you. Your system should give you momentum.

#2: Relationship Marketing Through E-mail and Social Media

Communicating with prospects and existing customers will likely be the number one demand on your time. And it should be because a SIMPLE business is based on people!

So you need to know how to manage your autoresponder system to automate the delivery of your messages. You need to know how to use sites like Twitter and Facebook to ensure your business is being represented authentically. And you should be investing some of your time reaching out to people with questions and answers in an interactive way. You can't afford to let others determine how your brand is perceived. Be in the forefront with online relationship marketing.

#3: Website Basics

You certainly don't need to become a graphic designer or full-fledged webmaster to succeed in your business. But if you don't know how to edit your web pages and create blog content, then you're going to waste a lot of money!

With software tools like WordPress driving modern websites, you truly have no real excuse to ignore this skill set.

One of the biggest challenges I've seen entrepreneurs face is finding themselves locked out of their own websites, or waiting for weeks for their webmaster to "get it right" with changes they've asked for. It's crucial that you know how to register your own domains and do basic things within your hosting account. Creating blog posts, uploading PDFs and other files to your site, and even checking your traffic stats are skills you'll always benefit from.

#4: Creating and Selling Information Products

A crucial part of the SIMPLE/Connect-Create-Collaborate model of business is creating and selling information products. This is how you can profit in this information golden age.

Creating free reports, hosting teleseminars, publishing e-books: these are easier than ever before to do yourself. And your speed of selling and delivering these types of products will make your customers raving fans.

Best of all, when you know how to create digital information products with low-cost tools and resources, you can realize high margins of profitability that your offline business friends will drool over!

#5: Affiliate Management

If you want to enjoy the accelerated growth that comes from the promotional efforts of your customers and your joint-venture partners, then setting up and running an affiliate program is essential.

The software systems used to track the sales and traffic being sent by your partners continue to improve both in features and in simplicity. Without these systems, you'll be relying solely on your own efforts. I imagine if this is where you are now, you feel like a hamster in its wheel, exhausting yourself with every revolution!

When you master this skill set, you'll have an automated system and sales team doing a lot of the heavy lifting for you.

Outsource These Skills at Your Peril

Although you can hire people to take care of these skills for you, ultimately you'll see better results if you have mastered them yourself. This way, you'll never be held hostage by a webmaster, employee, or virtual assistant who comes up short. You'll also avoid being taken advantage of by high-priced service providers who rely on your ignorance to charge you exorbitant fees.

To master all 5 of these internet marketing skills, learn from my training courses at:

- TakeActionReviseLater.com/library

17 5 Reasons to Create Your Own Information Product Now

Of the five internet marketing skills to master in the last chapter, the one that will have the biggest impact on the long term success of your business is the creation of information products.

You can create and release any number of products:

- teleseminar
- report or e-book
- video training series
- software
- home-study course
- simple audio program
- any combination of the above

But perhaps you need more convincing that creating a product is important. After all, maybe you're convinced that simply promoting other people's products (affiliate marketing, network marketing, etc.) is good enough.

Here are five reasons to create your own product now (in no particular order):

Be taken more seriously

I remember how differently I was treated at live events than other beginners, simply because I had created a product. Whether in person, or virtually, once you have your name on your own product, you become part of the action takers and get a lot further in conversations in your industry.

Build more reliable income

Once you have an information product, it can be sold any time, day or night, whether you are by your computer, at work, or even on vacation. I remember when I was still in the classroom how exciting it was to get paid for one of my products while I was administering a quiz to my history students. Once you have a product, you truly can make money while you sleep. You'll just work really hard while you're awake to make it into a full-time income.

Gain confidence in your business

If you're the kind of person who jumps from thing to shiny thing, creating a product will help focus your attention. This gives you confidence and direction because you'll have completed something that helps other people. Once you get a taste of that, you won't want to stop with just one product.

Attract affiliate partners to promote you

Perhaps the biggest benefit I've personally seen from having my own products is the realization that you can get other people to do a lot of promotional work for you. Once you have a product for sale, you can attach an automated referral system (also called an affiliate program) to it. And with the right incentives, your customers and affiliates from around the world can do the heavy lifting of sending you new customers.

It's easier to sell affiliate products (even MLM opportunities)

If you're an affiliate or network marketer right now, you probably see a big wall in front of you for making consistent sales. This is partly because you're selling something other people are selling, too. You have to stand out from the crowd by being someone people can trust. And a great way to build that trust is to give people something of value in exchange for money—even if it's just a few dollars. When people see you deliver more than you promise, they take your recommendations for other products more seriously. To this day, I earn at least 33 percent or so of my income from affiliate programs, including a few network-marketing companies.

I challenge you to create a basic information product within the next few weeks. Do it by creating a teleseminar, or putting together a short 10-15 page report.

To learn how to create your first teleseminar, visit:

- TakeActionReviseLater.com/teleseminars

To learn how to create your first free report or ebook, visit:

- TakeActionReviseLater.com/reports

18 Funding Your Business Through "Rapid Cash" Freelancing

I'm sure you've heard the phrase "It takes money to make money."

Are you finding that to be an obvious truth you've embraced and already used it to explode your business? Or is it a frustrating reality and challenge you can't seem to get past?

When you market your business online, there are certain expenses that you should be expecting.

Things like:

- Website hosting ($10/month)
- Autoresponders ($20/month and up)
- Graphics ($50–$300 per site)
- Support assistance ($100–$200/week)
- Transcription services ($90/teleseminar)
- Mentoring and training ($100–$1,000/month)

All those are important, and should really be considered investments in your business more than expenses.

But if your cash flow gets squeezed and you're not able to maintain, much less expand, what can you do?

Sometimes you have to bite the bullet and keep working in a soul-sucking day job a little bit longer than you'd like. And if you're currently out of work, you may be taking on some odd jobs that you feel are beneath your skill set.

Did you know there are ways to freelance online that can help you earn $100–$3000 in a matter of days?

These are definitely "time for dollars" tradeoffs, so I wouldn't recommend you focusing on them long-term. But when the need arises, they make for a good back-up plan.

Here's one of them:

There are websites where you can use your knowledge of your own material, experience, etc., and turn that into online content that people will pay for.

So for example, let's say you know a lot about tax preparation. And you've been trying to market a tax prep business. Well, you can write fifteen to twenty articles on this topic of about five hundred words each and sell that packet of articles on a particular website for $50.

Now you can do the math here: twenty articles for $50 is $2.50/article. Which is far less than minimum wage, right?

My first response is, if you need the $50, then it's still worthwhile.

But more importantly, look past the one-time sale. In reality, you really make the offer so that the package of articles can be sold for $50 to up to fifty people.

Well, now you're talking about earning $2,500 with the same twenty articles.

Of course, fifty people may not buy, but even if just ten did, then you're talking about $25/article instead.

Why would someone pay you for twenty articles?

First - it doesn't truly matter to you what their reason is. But if you're skeptical, here's why:

Webmasters all over the world rely on earning money from affiliate commissions, Google Adsense, and other forms of advertising. And they want good (doesn't have to be great) content on their site to attract visitors and revenue.

Second, some people like to put together your articles into a report or an e-book, and they'll take what you wrote, change it around a bit, and put it up for sale as a $19 e-book. Through their marketing efforts, they may turn that into a nice income for themselves (something you should ultimately be doing).

Finally, people like to take those articles and use them as their own autoresponder messages or make online videos out of reading them with some PowerPoint slides.

This is just one quick idea, and I'm sure you can think of a few others. I thank Paul Counts for teaching this lesson to me so I could share it with you.

To listen to me interview Rapid Cash teacher Paul Counts about these techniques, visit:

- TakeActionReviseLater.com/rapidcash

19

WOULD YOU RENT AN OFFICE FROM YOUR EMPLOYEE?

Imagine this scenario:

A business owner—let's call her Nicole—decides she needs to get an office. She doesn't want to buy space (for budget reasons or whatever) so she decides to rent.

One of her employees—let's call him Tom—happens to dabble in commercial real estate and has space to let. The office seems to fit all the criteria Nicole wants in an office: great location, affordable, good layout, already wired, and ready to go. She signs the lease for two years to get a great rate on the monthly rent.

They make some changes to the office, make it look even better by bringing in a feng shui expert and work-flow designer. They get new carpeting, install better lighting, and go to town on the signage for the lobby and outside the building.

Everything seems perfect until about three months later, when Tom starts showing up late to work. Nicole starts to notice that Tom's work is becoming shoddy. She meets with him, shares her observations. Tom agrees he's not been doing his best. He promises to improve.

For the next couple of weeks, it seems everything is back to normal. But then, Tom starts slipping up again.

Nicole reaches the conclusion that she has to let Tom go. She fires him on a Thursday afternoon.

Tom seems to take the news in stride. As it turns out, he's been moonlighting anyway at a different job that he's more energized about. His lack of focus and attention to Nicole's business was an obvious symptom of this. In fact, Tom's been working for one of Nicole's competitors.

What happens next probably won't surprise you.

As she learns more of Tom's work for her competitor, and realizes just how poor a job he's been doing for her, she gets increasingly more furious.

She can't sleep at night, and every day it seems she finds out some other way that Tom's actions, or lack thereof, really cost her business.

The next Wednesday, she's going through all the invoices, paying the bills, and running the numbers. One envelope gives her an instant migraine: it's the monthly rent payment notice on the office.

She realizes she's in month five of the two-year lease. She can't seem to shake the thought that even though that jerk Tom turned out to be a horrible employee, she still has to send him a substantial portion of her hard-earned money each month for another year and a half.

Nicole tries to reach Tom to break the lease, but her calls go unanswered. Her e-mails, even a certified letter, get terse replies that she's obligated under the contract to keep paying the monthly bill.

She decides that every time she goes to that office, her attitude and energy are so negative that it's affecting her work, her employees, and even how she deals with her clients. So Nicole looks for a new office. Even though she'll have to pay twice the rent, a change of environment is in order.

She finds a new office and starts the arduous process of moving. But most of the improvements they made to the office can't be removed.

Horrified, Nicole realizes that she's going to have to start virtually from scratch with the new place. Months of her business and thousands of dollars in workplace design and expenses have been flushed down the drain.

It takes another year for Nicole to generate the additional revenue to pay for this mistake. She barely survives the situation, coming close to shutting the doors forever several times.

Fortunately, this story is fictional; although I'm sure there are situations like this that happen.

So what's the point of this story?

Obviously, you shouldn't rent an office from an employee—which I'm sure you already knew. And there's a good chance you don't really care because you work from home, right?

But this is exactly the same kind of mistake business owners are doing with their online offices, i.e., their websites.

I see this happen way too often, and I hope it won't happen to you. I can guarantee you that at some point in your business, you will fire your webmaster. As a former webmaster myself, and now an internet marketing teacher and consultant, I don't know a single person in business who hasn't had to change their webmaster at least once.

And yet, **most business owners who hire a webmaster are actually renting their virtual office from them.** Sure, a webmaster is typically not an employee in the IRS terminology, but they do work for you. And the way webmasters make most of their money is by the monthly, or annual, web hosting bill they add onto their services.

Just like Nicole and Tom's situation above, things usually start out working really well. But eventually, the customer load of the webmaster makes your site less and less a priority to them. When you get fed up enough, you will want to fire them and move to someone else who can give you more attention.

At that point, you'll have a serious problem because you won't be able to move your website easily to the new webmaster. In a worst-case scenario, the webmaster you fire can change all the account settings, disable your website, and essentially shut down your business. And if you registered your domain name with them, you may never be able to get it unlocked and put in your name.

So how can you protect yourself from a scenario like this destroying all your efforts of building up your online business?

Control Your Own Hosting

First, control your own hosting instead of falling for the so-called convenience of using your webmaster's hosting. Many webmasters will try to convince you of letting them host your site, but you need to stand firm on this.

Plus, when you control your own hosting account, you'll probably pay less than what they're charging you, and if anything like the scenario above happens, you're in control of the accounts.

Register Your Own Domains

Second, be sure to be the one that registers your own domains. Some webmasters will register domains under their company name instead of yours, or use privacy settings that essentially lock you out of the picture. If you ever want to take control of your domains, you'll have a terrible time getting what you want because you will have lost any real points of leverage.

Set Up Separate Admin Access

Third, when you hire a webmaster or virtual assistant to help you with your website, give them a separate administrative level account that you can terminate if necessary. Don't just give them your username and password to your accounts if you can avoid it. At the very least, create a new temporary password that you can change easily if something goes wrong.

Know Enough to Get by in a Pinch

Fourth, learn how to manage your own website. You don't have to become an HTML junkie or understand all the PHP, MySQL mumbo jumbo. That stuff you can get help with. But learn how to make changes to your site, to upload your own files, to set up your own e-mail accounts, etc. You can learn how to do all this and more at my site, Discover cPanel. This way, if you do ever find yourself between webmasters or virtual assistants, or simply in a time crunch where they aren't available, you'll still be able to run your business.

The bottom line is, having your websites locked up in the hands of your webmaster is just like renting an office from an employee. It'll start out problem free. But eventually, you're more than likely going to have some serious headaches down the road.

Be in control of your website so you don't throw time and money down the drain! Learn how to register your domain and set up your own hosting account at:

- TakeActionReviseLater.com/webmaster

20

GET CONTROL
OVER E-MAIL

Beyond the typical spam, my inbox gets increasingly filled every week with two types of e-mails from people I usually want to hear from: (a) invitations to promote their new product, or (b) e-mails from their partners promoting those products.

Even though I'd love to help them out and learn from all the great products that get released, I have to draw the line somewhere.

On top of those e-mails, I also have to pay attention to messages from vendors, elevated support requests from my virtual assistant—and then there's friends and family, too.

Here's how I try to handle the e-mail overload.

Use Gmail Accounts

First, I have more than one e-mail account. I have a Gmail account that I rarely give out, and I don't use it to subscribe to any new lists. So this e-mail account helps me get the e-mails I really must get: communicate with my support desk, Paypal communication, family, and mastermind partners. Top-level clients of mine also have this e-mail address.

Then I have several other e-mail accounts (also with Gmail) that are used to subscribe to most of the lists, product registrations, etc. These e-mail accounts are important to gain access to in order to confirm registration of a product or subscription, and then to look at a few times per week at particular times of the day. My virtual assistant checks this account more than I do and forwards any pressing messages that I need to see.

The reason I use Gmail and not other free services (or even my own server) is because of its smarter spam filtering and search function. The customized filtering of Gmail is also a big plus.

Set Up Filters for Automatic Prioritizing

You can use Gmail's filter system to tag e-mails from specific people or sent to a specific address, even if they are being received by the same account. For example, all messages that have the phrase "To unsubscribe or change subscriber options visit:" I mark as "mailing list" because that's what popular autoresponder services put at the bottom of any e-mail its members send out. I know that these messages are not sent to me personally, and therefore won't require an immediate response.

Likewise, e-mails from my support-desk virtual assistant are labeled "help desk" and they get a higher priority.

I recommend that you use a similar system. And then set up two or three other e-mail accounts that you check on an occasional basis. Set up filters that make the most sense to you.

Unsubscribing Is Allowed

Now, once you have your e-mails filtered, regularly unsubscribe from those lists that you no longer feel fit your needs. Do this about once per month. If you purchased a product, you may want to change the e-mail address for that specific list to one of your alternative accounts.

But for those free newsletters that hinder your productivity more than grow your business, go ahead and unsubscribe. You can always pick up their tips again at a future time. Don't feel like you're going to miss out on anything really important—you have enough on your plate already.

When you do this e-mail cleanse once per month, it should leave you with just a few newsletters from the people you get the most value from. And you'll find a lot more time again in your calendar.

You should also schedule your e-mail time and stick to that routine. You may need to experiment with times that work best for you. But twice per day should be a sufficient frequency to work with e-mail.

The important thing here is that when you do e-mail, you focus 100 percent of your attention on it. Get in and get out. And when it's not e-mail time, you avoid it 100 percent. Do not leave your e-mail program open when it's not e-mail time. Those pop-up notifications of new e-mails are a bane to your work productivity.

21

ADVERTISE YOUR COMPANY—
NOT SOMEBODY ELSE'S—
WITH EVERY E-MAIL

Seven out of ten business cards I get from fellow business owners are advertising Yahoo, Hotmail, Comcast, or some other company—but not their own.

Are you making this rookie mistake? Did you know there is an easy alternative?

To make it simple host your site with a company that provides you with a cPanel® dashboard system (such as PoweredByHostgator. com). This makes it easy to manage your website.

You can then set up a you@yourdomain.com type of e-mail account. I recommend you forward that e-mail to Gmail (see the previous chapter) for actually reading through your messages. But now you can advertise your website with every e-mail that you send.

Plus your business cards will look a lot more professional!

For a free video showing you how to set up your own e-mail account, visit...

- TakeActionReviseLater.com/dcp

CREATE QUICK VIDEOS AT A MOMENT'S NOTICE FOR BUSINESS EXPOSURE

Do you ever go to a live meeting with other professionals in your industry, or with professionals with similar motivations?

These meetings are a great way to meet new people, learn some marketing ideas, etc.

But they are also a great opportunity to make products and content for your audience. When you go to a seminar, conference, workshop, or local meeting, bring along your video camera.

You can use any video camera you can get your hands on (even many digital cameras have a video feature), but I personally love using the Flip Ultra HD (www.BuyAFlip.com).

Now the question you likely will have is: what would I do a video about?

At a conference in April, 2009, I attended a workshop with Perry Lawrence and Carrie Wilkerson. They suggested seven different types of video series you could do, and the one I thought was the easiest was the FAQ video series.

This is where you take those questions you get asked about all the time, and you make a short one- to three-minute video about each question.

See an example of a FAQ video series at:

- TakeActionReviseLater.com/faqvideos

Notice how there's nothing fancy going on about the video. It's cool that I was next to a pool on a sunny day in California, but we had no fancy equipment, lighting, or anything professional. The point Perry told me was keep your videos informal, concise, and helpful to the viewer.

Carrie and Perry took advantage of the event and created an information product in about an hour. Not only that, they also filmed testimonials and helped the rest of us create content, too. They didn't have to spend countless hours alone doing this project. And the results are awesome.

You can see the results at WebVideoMagnetism.com.

The big picture I want you to learn from this is when you get to an event, bring your camera along and take advantage of the opportunity.

Events help you focus on your business away from the distractions of your office. Plus, you're often surrounded by like-minded people. They can help you film and brainstorm your content. Bring in a recognized guest to appear in your videos to add even more to your credibility.

23

BUSINESS BRANDING THROUGH TESTIMONIALS

So you want to catch the attention of the leading experts in your industry, right? And you want people to visit your website without having to pay for the traffic.

One way to do that is by giving a great testimonial for the products, services, and mentoring most connected to your field.

Let me explain why sharing your testimonial helps you just as much (or more) than the product owner.

A testimonial is a review (generally very positive—but genuinely so) of a product or service that is displayed on the sales pages, in e-mails, and even inside of the product being sold. These are a big help to the customer who wants to hear from real people how the product or service helped them out. It helps them make up their mind to buy or not.

Of course, some people swear that testimonials have no effect on their buying habits whatsoever. And it is true that a very small minority of people showcase completely fabricated testimonials.

But the social proof element of persuasion is powerful for 98 percent of the population, and authentic testimonials are the norm.

You'll get three major benefits from giving testimonials:

- Exposure
- Attention
- Revenue

Big Benefit #1: Exposure

The first and perhaps biggest benefit you have to providing a great testimonial is its inclusion in somebody else's marketing materials online. Imagine your name, website (usually unlinked), picture, and comments being displayed on the sales letter for a top product in your field.

As that sales letter gets thousands of visitors each week, you're getting exposure that you do not have to pay for.

And as you increase the number of testimonials you provide, the target marketplace will continue to see you popping up. This is a critical element of branding, and it can have powerful results for you.

Hold your space on this page, and look at the testimonials on the first pages of this book. These people are getting introduced to you and to everyone else who picks up this book. Perhaps they had an influence on you getting this book. And perhaps one of their websites will catch your attention for further connections.

Big Benefit #2: Gain Attention

A second big benefit is you pop up on the radar of the product owner more quickly. For the leaders in your industry, it may be difficult to catch their attention with so many others clamoring for awareness. Provide a great testimonial, and you'll get noticed by the product owner, even if they don't include it right away on their website. This can be the start of a longer-term relationship that can lead to affiliate teleseminars, reciprocal promotion, or to becoming a more extensive case study for that product for even more exposure.

Big Benefit #3: Affiliate Revenue

An often overlooked idea of giving testimonials is the effect your on-page endorsement will have for your audience for products you recommend through an affiliate relationship.

If you recommend a product to your own list of subscribers and customers, and your testimonial is good, you'll typically have better results.

This means more affiliate revenue for you, and an even stronger relationship with your audience, who continue to trust you more and more for recommending quality, results-based products and services.

3 Ways to Give a Great Testimonial

Now, not all testimonials are created equal, and product owners are actually quite selective, usually when it comes to which to actually include in their marketing materials. Savvy business owners know that a poorly made testimonial can actually hurt sales, even if it's a positive review.

There are basically three types of testimonials that get noticed.

- Before-After-After-That
- Highly Dimensionalized
- Objection Overcomer

The first is a "Before-After-After-That" testimonial. Basically, you briefly tell your background before using the product. Typically, you'll identify a major pain, confusion, or doubt you had about succeeding or reaching a goal. Then you explain what happened immediately after you experienced the product in question. This is usually conjecture of what you'll now be able to do with this information.

The After That portion is the kicker that most people don't do. This is where you explain what you accomplished after applying the training over a period of time (usually a month or more).

The second type of great testimonial is a highly dimensionalized result—meaning there is clearly a major change that occurred. And the change happened quickly and measurably.

This could be a monetary, time, or body transformation that is easy to describe or demonstrate.

The third type of testimonial is called an Objection Overcomer. This is where you give a testimonial that directly answers an objection a person would typically have about buying a product.

Common objections are: not having enough time, not having enough money, it won't work for me, etc.

So for example, let's say you wanted to do a testimonial for Discover Social Networking, and you know that a common objection about Twitter and Facebook is people think they are a big waste of time.

You might create your great testimonial about how before learning the lessons in DSN, you thought social networks were a big waste of time. But once you were taught the strategic methods inside the course, you now know how to spend just ten to fifteen minutes a day to build stronger relationships with your growing "tribe" of followers who are now your raving fans and ambassadors.

Great Testimonial Example

Here's an example of an objection-overcoming testimonial from someone who answers the objection "I already know enough about this..."

> *"Thank you for another high quality class. I thought that I knew a lot about Twitter—but my clients and I were not getting the results that we wanted. By applying what I learned during the class, I already have 50 new, high quality followers on Twitter and I am having a lot more fun building relationships."*

Meredith Eisenberg
TameTheInternetMonster.com

So consider all the reasons you "almost" didn't buy a product. Create a testimonial for that specific objection, and how you now know what the truth is about that objection.

As you can see, giving great testimonials is not just about saying how much you loved a product. It has to be written in such a way to persuade a reader to buy because they recognize something about you in them.

And as you do this, you'll find those readers won't just gravitate toward the products, they'll gravitate toward you, as well.

If you'd like to test out your new knowledge of giving a great testimonial, and perhaps get more exposure for your name, website, etc., review Take Action Revise Later. You can do any of the three types above, or even submit multiple versions if you like, and I'll pick the one that I like best. I suggest that you use the audio and picture upload options as well, for even more influential reviews.

If you're really ambitious, record a video and upload it to YouTube with the tag TARL. I'll include the best ones on the Take Action Revise Later website.

Take a look again at the back cover of this book, and the first few pages where I've included testimonials. Use these as examples of how to endorse a product while also getting exposure for you and your website.

As you get results from other products of mine or of anyone else, be sure to send in a testimonial each and every time for more exposure and influence.

And special thanks to my mentor, Paulie Sabol, for teaching me these concepts so I could share them with you.

Get traffic with your own review of this book:

- TakeActionReviseLater.com/review

24

Attend Live Events for Increased Visibility, Status, and Access to Your Industry's Inner Circle

The first internet marketing seminar I attended had a tremendous impact on my business. But I almost didn't go.

I was still working full-time in the classroom. It wasn't easy to take off work. In all ten years in the classroom I missed a total of eleven days!

But something in my gut told me that I needed to get there. I had been trying to get going with my internet marketing business and was slowly gaining traction. This was in September of 2006. I had invested about $3,000 in mentoring at that point, another $4,000 in wasted Adwords, and lots of little expenses on e-books and gizmos that added up to a lot, especially on my teaching salary.

Fortunately, the event—The Internet Marketing Main Event II—was in Baltimore. Literally 15 minutes from my house. If it hadn't been so close, I would have let any number of excuses get in my way of going.

Boy, would that have been a tragic mistake!.

Going into that first event I had made a bit of progress. I had created my first information product, Free Ad Report. I didn't have a blog yet, and I was not seeing steady income. My list was about 1,000 people (from FAR).

I'm sure I looked like a deer in the headlights when I walked in the room.

For the previous six months, I had been getting mentoring from Paulie Sabol, Donna Fox, Mike Filsaime, and Tom Beal in the i5 Gold program. I had been active on a couple of forums, and I was excited that many of the others would be there.

Throughout the event, I told anyone who would listen how excited I was about my big idea: helping other teachers make money online through TeachersInBusiness.com. In that crowd, I got a lot of smiles and nods, but few shared my enthusiasm for the project.

In fact, a couple of people pointed out to me that, a) my target market didn't spend a lot of money; and b) I hadn't made much money myself, so how would I be able to teach that to other teachers?

This was my first run-in with the credibility gap that cripples so many business opportunity seekers.

As the weekend progressed, I listened to over a dozen speakers. Needless to say, with people like Rich Schefren, Jeff Walker, Deb and JP Micek, and others, it was an overwhelming amount of information. I took a ton of notes. And I felt like I squeezed in about a year's worth of learning into that one weekend.

But to be honest, that's not what I remember the most. And looking back at the actual training, the sessions are pretty much a big blur.

What I remember most are the people I met in between the sessions and at the dinner table.

I remember how awesome it felt to be in a room with a bunch of people who really understood what I was trying to do: striking out into the world of entrepreneurship, having a vision of a better lifestyle, better income, and having the overwhelming uncertainty of how it would all unfold.

Back at work, whenever I'd try to talk about online business stuff, my coworkers just wouldn't get it. Most were skeptical, and the moment I stopped my sentence, many would be pretty dismissive of the whole idea.

But inside that conference room that weekend, I was surrounded by peers who wanted to see me succeed.

And it wasn't just the other people there like me, at the starting gate.

The speakers, too, were genuinely rooting for me and the others there.

Specifically, I remember meeting Joel Comm. I had been active inside his Adsense Secrets forum for a couple of months before the event. But I never figured he would know who I was. I quickly learned how memorable the *Bob The Teacher* name was, because he not only recognized me, he spent significant time with me throughout the event brainstorming my next steps. When we met up again a few months later, he saw the progress I had made and agreed to promote Squidoo Secrets during the launch. This proved to be a major turning point in the profitability and growth of my business.

I also connected with a few other guys who had been hanging out in the i5Gold forums and participating in the coaching calls. You may recognize some of their names now: Glen Hopkins, Dan Kelly, Scott Tousignant, Martin Salter, Tim Brocklehurst, and Matthew Glanfield. There were others, too, but toward the end of the event, the seven of us decided to form a mastermind team.

This was a totally unexpected result of going to the live event. But it was the most profitable outcome.

The truth is, I could have learned everything the speakers taught during the event somewhere else—on teleseminars, in their home study courses, etc.

But I would have never made the connections or formed the partnerships that have been at the heart of my success, if I had not gone to that live event.

Because of those connections:

- I held my first six teleseminars within forty-five days of that event.
- I had a cheering squad keeping me focused on completing projects.
- My mastermind team helped me realize how limiting the school setting was for me—without their help, I might still be in the classroom.

- We promoted each other to our growing subscriber base, "lifting all boats."
- We partnered up on a few projects together.

Eventually, Scott and I became accountability partners. I know I wouldn't be half as far along in my business without his kicks-in-the-ass every week!

So obviously, my point in bringing you down memory lane is to impress upon you the importance of attending a live event. You'll be amazed at how spending a short amount of time in an intense environment can have such a long-term impact on your business.

For a list of internet marketing events I'm attending, teaching, or hosting, visit:

- TakeActionReviseLater.com/events

25

5 SECRETS TO MAGNIFICENT RESULTS WITH A MASTERMIND

"Analyze the record of any [person] who has accumulated a great fortune, and many of those who have accumulated modest fortunes, and you will find that they have either consciously, or unconsciously employed the 'Master Mind' principle."

Napoleon Hill

Want to know how you can speed up your success with your business? Get together with five to seven other people who all want to help each other grow their businesses. This is called a mastermind team, and it's like hiring a handful of mentors but usually doesn't cost anything.

There are several keys to success with a mastermind.

1. Meet on a regular basis
2. Have a clear agenda
3. Help each other between meetings
4. Collaborate on mutually beneficial projects

Let me give you some tips on each of these areas.

Frequent and Consistent Mastermind Meetings

Whether you meet in person or on the phone, it's important that you do so consistently and on a frequent basis. Some mastermind teams meet once per month, others once per week. Pick a schedule that's perfect for your group, where attendance will always be high.

The schedule should be known well in advance, and that time slot should be considered a top priority for all members.

You can meet in person at a local restaurant, or on the phone with people around the world.

Have a Clear Agenda

Masterminds that fall apart usually do so because there's little perceived benefit for the members. And this is typically caused by a lack of structure in the meetings. Without an agenda, the mastermind session turns into a meandering conversation. And those typically result in little actually being achieved.

Set an agenda and make sure that agenda is known either a day or so before, or presented as the very first item of business.

I was taught this agenda by my own mentors Donna Fox and Paulie Sabol:

- Say what you're grateful for from the previous week
- Tell the group a very brief success story from the week before, or follow up from last week's step 5 (see below).
- Identify a trouble area you'd like specific help with
- Shut up and listen as your mastermind team members give you their feedback
- Announce one major action step you are going to take between this and the next mastermind meeting.

Each person takes turns with this agenda for about seven minutes. With a group of six, this will take most of an hour-long meeting.

The remaining time in the hour can be used for sharing a specific business tip on a topic you identified the week before.

For example, during the last ten minutes of a session, each person could identify their favorite traffic source, or a golden nugget they picked up in a book they are reading, etc.

The gold in the mastermind team is not what's specifically being said during the meeting, but the accountability of being there, saying what you're going to do, and then doing it. If you drop the ball, you have to face the group the next time feeling guilty. This is peer pressure in its most profitable form!

Help a Mastermind Partner Between Meetings

The third secret to a good mastermind team is to connect with one or more of the other members between meetings. Just a quick phone call or e-mail to see how they're coming along on their action step can be a great motivator. Or perhaps something comes up that is a more urgent issue that can't wait until the next meeting. Just getting some quick feedback on an idea can save a lot of time, money, and unnecessary headaches.

I often find just hearing myself explain an issue makes the solution appear right in front of my face.

Be careful not to abuse your mastermind partners with too many requests for help, though. They have a business to run, just like you. So be sure to use your mastermind lifelines sparingly. But do use them—a good mastermind team wants to help.

Collaborate on Mutually Beneficial Projects

One of the best ways for a mastermind team to elevate each other's businesses is to work on a joint project together. This can take the form of a joint venture product, a cosponsored advertisement, or a series of teleseminars interviewing each other in the area of expertise.

When you work on something together, you multiply your efforts. And usually the result is greater than $1 + 1 = 2$. It's more like $1 + 1 = 11$.

In the internet marketing world, this can also take the form of thank-you page ad swaps, where you put each other's information products as recommended resources.

You can also get more traffic to your web properties (like your blog, Squidoo lenses, etc.), by having each member in your group use social bookmarking, RSS, blog comments and other Web 2.0 strategies to multiply the visibility of what you collectively offer.

Get Started with Your Own Mastermind

Now the question remains, where do you find such a mastermind team? Look where you already are:

- Who else attended the same seminar you did that seemed to just click with you? My own mastermind team started out of a seminar in Baltimore in September, 2006.
- Who else is in your local chamber of commerce or networking/ referral groups?
- Who do you talk to all the time on Twitter and Facebook, or in particular forums?
- Who else bought the same coaching program or learning product? For example, I encourage my students who take my internet marketing courses to form mastermind teams.

You can also use Meetup.com to find a group in your local area to meet with in person. Some are better than others, and they often take a bit of time for you to get results.

Wherever you find them, give masterminding a try for three months before you bring in your verdict. It will likely take you about six meetings before your team really gets into its groove.

If you're like me, you'll quickly find your team members to be an instrumental part of your business. In fact, your mastermind team should be as essential to you as the computer you work on every day.

For more help with masterminding, visit:

- TakeActionReviseLater.com/masterminds

26

7 DEADLY MISTAKES THAT WILL KILL YOUR BUSINESS

If you're wearing most of the hats in your business, you'll want to avoid these 7 mistakes like the plague. Doing any one of these will stop you dead in your tracks. Unfortunately, many entrepreneurs are doing most if not all of these!

#1: Don't Have a System

One of the dreams entrepreneurs want is to "make money while they sleep." The only way to do that is to have systems in place that run 24/7.

If you do not have a system, you'll always find yourself inside a perpetual hamster wheel of activity. Without some amount of automation in place, or a predictable routine, you will find yourself doing things in a very haphazard way. Not only is this chaotic, it's overwhelming and unprofitable.

When you have a system, you know what's happening from point A to point B. The process required to complete tasks, produce products, and deliver services becomes predictable. With a system in place, you remove yourself from being the bottleneck in your business. If circumstances arise in your life external to your control, your business will still be able to function.

So things like email communication, product creation, selling and delivering your products online, even scheduling meetings can turn into a system.

#2: See Your Competition as the Enemy

Most business owners think of themselves like 1 of 2 competing gas station owners on a street corner. When they lower their prices on unleaded, you feel compelled to do the same thing. When you start offering certain products, they react by copying your tactics. It's cutthroat competition.

I want you to expand your business landscape to a much larger area. The internet allows you to do this because you can literally be selling your services and products to people far beyond your zip code.

You should also realize that for you to win, somebody else does not have to lose. You can co-exist with your competition in such a way that you can all serve your marketplace profitably.

Instead of enemies, think of your competitors as potential collaborators. For you to succeed in your business long term, you're going to have to reach out to competitors and find ways to work together. Support one another with referrals, brainstorm ideas of best practices, and realize that each of you actually serve the marketplace in different, but needed ways.

You will also find out that each of you has a specialty that sets you apart from the other. That difference will help you attract different customers and clients. Imagine for example 2 competing chiropractors who decide to specialize separately in golfers vs. tennis players, based on their own personal preference of playing those sports and their ability to relate to their patients.

My second internet marketing training product showed me this could be quite profitable. Discover Mini-Sites involved a training session I did with another website teacher, Dan Kelly. Since I was already a webmaster for a little while I didn't need to include Dan on this project. But the collaboration allowed me to create a product in a shorter amount of time, while generating significant revenue for both of us. And in the end, our customers benefited the most from our combined expertise.

As you collaborate, you'll see faster growth than working alone. You'll also have more fun. And you'll likely see a remarkable transformation in your marketplace: instead of the pie getting chopped up into little pieces to fight over, your collaboration will result in a much bigger pie to share together.

#3: Try to Do It All Yourself

The third deadly mistake entrepreneurs are making is trying to do too much of the work themselves. While you should know how pieces of your business work, you should follow this mantra:

"Do what you do best, and outsource the rest!"

You should be doing things that you're really good at and that generate the most revenue for you. The remaining work can be done by others faster and perhaps better than you would do it yourself. This frees up your time for high-profit activities and more time off if you want it.

Perhaps you've heard the economic term comparative advantage. In essence, this means that each person or business has areas of operation where they have a comparative advantage over another person or company. When you know where your comparative advantages are, you can make better choices concerning what actions you actually take yourself, and which you pass off to other people.

Sure, you may be good at talking to people on the phone. But if answering phones takes you away from doing something else you're even better at, it doesn't truly help you. Meanwhile, someone with great phone skills but mediocre strategic planning would be better than you as your receptionist.

Personally, I learned this lesson when I first outsourced graphic design for one of my websites. Since I had experience as a webmaster, my skills in design are definitely above average. But I listened to a mentor and chose the design of Teachers In Business to be the first project where I hired someone else to do something I knew how to do well.

I was amazed at how perfectly this worked out.

Instead of me taking at least four hours doing this new website, it took him about 35 minutes to do the graphics. Even better, I was able to use that time to work on making my product better. Almost by magic, the graphics just appeared.

What aren't you doing enough of that extra time on-task would increase your profits? What are you normally doing that someone else can do faster and better than you, to free up that time?

#4: Operate in Reaction Mode

The fourth mistake struggling business owners make is operating in reaction mode. They're acting in a place where instead of doing things proactively, instead of doing things that they have a strategic game plan for, they're simply responding to what's being thrown at them. This results in frustration, demoralization, and no progress.

If it seems like you move one step forward and two steps back, this may be an issue for you, too.

E-mail is a great example. If it's the first thing you open up on your computer, you spend the first three hours of the day reading, responding, deleting, checking out recommendations, looking for the next biggest thing. By the time the day is half way over you feel like you have nothing accomplished.

Be proactive about your business. Set a plan for the week or for the month and stick to it. Set up a schedule of actions and hold yourself accountable to following through. Revise as necessary, of course. But the more forward thinking you can operate, the more productive you will be.

Otherwise you'll drown in a sea of overwhelm.

With a proactive outlook, you will also make better decisions. Knowing where you're headed and the path you are on gives you permission to say no to everything that doesn't fit the plan. And you'll likely find that others will say yes to you more often when they see this focused determination.

#5: Lack Confidence and Giving Up Too Soon on Your Business

How many times have you started something with great intentions, but then gave up on it too soon? Without confidence in what you're doing, and the patience and persistence to finish what you start, your business is doomed to mediocrity.

It's hard to have confidence when your business is struggling, especially when you're in your first year or two of operating. But you have to have faith in what you're doing and how important your success is to your customers.

This doesn't mean put blinders on, and beat your horse for three years without evaluating your progress. But you must have a balance in your mind between steadfast confidence and revising your path based on actual feedback from your market.

As you set your mindset towards success, no matter what, you'll resist the temptation to quit. In order for you to win in business, you have to push all the way to the finish line. As you complete each stage of your business, your confidence will continue to grow.

"Success seems to be connected with action. Successful people keep moving. They make mistakes, but they don't quit."

Conrad Hilton

#6: Don't Focus on Leveraged Activities

Leverage simply means getting more out of an activity than the effort it took to create it.

Another way to look at it is this: what's the expiration date on the actions you take? If the effect of your actions lasts as long as a peeled banana stays fresh, then you are not using leverage.

Most service professionals operate in this way. Do a job, get paid. Stop working and you don't get paid. Whether you're paid on commission or on an hourly basis, you're still living in the time for dollars trap.

Another consequence of ignoring leverage is becoming a victim of your own success. If you suddenly got 20 people or 200 people or 2000 more people to do business with you, as you currently operate, would you be able to handle it? Or would you get crushed by that amount of work?

Contrast this with leveraged activities.

Leverage also plays a role in your marketing budget. Let's say you want to buy advertising on the Internet, on TV, radio, newspaper, or in the Yellow Pages? You can easily spend $500-$5,000 on advertising in this kind of a way. Once the ad runs, it's gone forever.

Instead of spending your money on advertising, create marketing materials that continue to work for you online. Have a writer create 10 articles or an e-book for you based on your expertise. Use viral marketing methods to have that content disseminated across the Internet.

Or record an audio program, have it transcribed, and turn it into an affordable lead generation product. Not only will it create a new revenue stream for you, it can become a fantastic qualifier for you to only work with high quality customers.

Another example is leveraging your email. You can use an autoresponder service like Aweber (BestEmailDelivery.com) to set up a series of messages that are delivered to every new person that signs up for your information online. Instead of manually emailing your customers personally as requests come in, the autoresponder does it for you on a schedule you pre-determine. Instead of committing the sin of mass carbon-copy (CC) messaging, you can use the autoresponder system to broadcast messages to subscribers individually.

And when you receive questions via email, turn your answers into a knowledgebase on your website. The next time somebody asks a similar question, you can point them to this Frequently Asked Questions page!

Leverage also means magnifying your efforts through the energy of others. Instead of finding 100 blogs to post an article on, why not give that same article to 100 affiliate partners who can publish it on their sites for you?

Finally, if you are coaching clients, consider working with small groups instead of just one-on-one. Record your sessions so they can refer back to the audio any time they wish, instead of emailing you with the same questions three days later.

#7: Don't Get Expert Help on a Regular Basis

With so much information online today, it's easy to believe that all the answers we need to our business challenges are available for free.

But if you truly want to accelerate the success of your business, you must invest in expert help. Obviously this may seem a bit self-serving coming from a business acceleration coach, but it's critical that you stop trying to figure it all out on your own.

For one thing, your customers can't continue to wait while you learn how to market your products and services.

On the other hand, if you are only learning from free lessons on YouTube or a trainer's free report, then you're basing your business on other people's marketing materials.

Cobbling together free information online will not give you the big picture you need, nor will it reveal the higher level strategies and tactics gurus actually use most profitably.

When you identify a specific gap in your business, seek out the specialist who can help you overcome that challenge quickly. And if you can't see those gaps, find a coach who knows how to ask the right kinds of questions to shed light on areas outside of your view.

Hopefully, you aren't doing too many of these mistakes. If you can eliminate them altogether, I guarantee you'll enjoy your business and its rewards a lot more!

27

PICK THE RIGHT MENTOR

Nothing dooms your success like thinking you can do it all yourself, that you have all the answers, or that you should do it your way so you can be unique in the marketplace.

Trust me—I used these excuses myself for quite a long time before recognizing that it pays to have a mentor. Early on, I thought, "I have a master's degree from THE Johns Hopkins University, for crying out loud—I shouldn't need help!" But several thousand dollars later in wasted spending and bad turns in business opened my eyes to the truth.

I also remember it hitting me very clearly: Even Roger Federer relied on the help of coaches to become the greatest tennis player of all time. So did basketball great Michael Jordan and golf legend Annika Sorenstam.

Sure, mentoring typically costs money, but so does any education worth pursuing. But unlike sitting in classrooms where you don't really connect with the professor or get to ask in-depth questions that pertain to YOUR issue at hand, today's mentors are there for you—if they know what they're doing, anyway.

They can help you see things you are too close to observe. They can share their real experiences.

When I was a kid, being the youngest of four in a house where grounding was a weekly ritual, I came up with a personal philosophy:

> *"Smart people learn from their mistakes. Smarter*
> *people learn from other people's mistakes."*
>
> Bob Jenkins

And the same is true for hiring a business coach.

So early in 2006, I hired four mentors—Paulie Sabol, Donna Fox, Mike Filsaime, and Tom Beal—and paid them $500/month to teach me how to grow an internet marketing based business. It took me five months to make my first dollar from their teaching, as I was working full-time, and not completely committed to patiently implementing their recommendations. But after making the first few dollars, I quickly earned my first $1,000 week. And it wasn't long after when I had my first $1,000 day.

The profits that have resulted from taking action on what they taught me and their help steering me in the right direction made that investment better than any stock pick, real-estate property pick up, or precious metal I could have spent money on instead.

Once you're committed to working with a mentor, you'll want answers to these eight questions:

1. Are they successful doing what you want to do?
2. Do they know why they are successful (accidental success stories are horrible at replicating their success!)?
3. Are they able to connect you with the right resources to move forward fast with an obvious path to profit?
4. Do they hold you accountable to follow-through with your commitments?
5. Have you been successful using their existing products?
6. Are current clients satisfied with their progress?
7. Can they pinpoint your exact constraints and obstacles and prescribe a solution you can implement?
8. Do they allow you to ask specific questions that pertain to your needs so you can fulfill them fast?

You can find mentors and business coaches in your local community, or work with one virtually online.

Regardless of who you choose to help you, I hope you will pursue mentoring as part of your business budget. Hiring a mentor will help you faster than any book or home-study course you'd ever put your hands on.

To evaluate my mentoring program, visit:

- TakeActionReviseLater.com/coaching

A RECOMMENDED READING

These books influenced my business in fundamental ways. They are my favorite books to recommend to others pursuing their dreams through their own business.

- *Influence: The Psychology of Persuasion*, Robert B Cialdini
- *Purple Cow: Transform Your Business by Being Remarkable*, Seth Godin
- *The Great Formula: for Creating Maximum Profit with Minimal Effort*, Mark Joyner
- *Confessions of an Online Marketer: The Seven Secrets Millionaire Marketers Use to Effortlessly Attract More Money*, Glen Hopkins
- *Secrets Of Online Persuasion*, John-Paul Micek and Deborah Micek
- *Tipping Point: How Little Things Can Make a Big Difference*, Malcolm Gladwell
- *Twitter Revolution: How Social Media and Mobile Marketing is Changing the Way We Do Business & Market Online*, Warren Whitlock and Deborah Micek

- *Cash in on Communication*, Felicia Slattery

For an updated reading list, and to find these books online, please visit:

- TakeActionReviseLater.com/books

B

RECOMMENDED INTERNET MARKETING RESOURCES

Promoting your business online can be quite daunting and frustrating if you try to do it by yourself. To make it easier, learn the big picture strategies and the step-by-step methods I teach on my blog, in my online courses, and at my live seminars.

The following list will get you going in the specific areas you wish to master first.

My blog and lessons via email: **AskBobTheTeacher.com**

My live business acceleration bootcamp: **SIMPLE10k.com**

My group and private coaching programs, plus all the courses you see below: **IMSuccessLibrary.com**

Specific internet marketing courses:

- Aweber Autoresponder—BestEmailDelivery.com
- Hostgator Website Hosting—PoweredByHostgator.com
- Website Domain Registration—Shylar.com
- Blogging Software And Marketing System— QuansiteSystem.com
- Internet Marketing Tutorials—IMSuccessLibrary.com
- Digital Access Pass Membership and Affiliate Management System—PoweredByDAP.com

For an updated resource list, and to find these resources online, please visit:

- TakeActionReviseLater.com/resources

C

MORE TRAINING FROM BOB THE TEACHER

- AskBobTheTeacher.com
- SIMPLE10K.com
- IMSuccessLibrary.com
- TeleseminarFormula.com
- DiscoverFreemind.com
- DiscoverAutoresponders.com
- DiscoverDigitalAccessPass.com
- DiscoverButterflyMarketing.com
- DiscovercPanel.com
- DiscoverProductCreation.com
- DiscoverSocialNetworking.com
- IMFAQ.com
- SquidooSecrets.com
- TwitterSeduction.com
- CreateYourOwnAffiliateProgram.com
- FreeAdReport.com

ACKNOWLEDGMENTS

This is the page where I get to give a few shout-outs to those that have been instrumental to the success of my business and the publication of *TAKE ACTION! Revise Later*. As your favorite politicians would say, and in true TARL fashion, I reserve the right to revise and extend my remarks because I know I'll leave someone out.

This book is in your hands thanks in large part to 2 people: Donna Kozik, who gave me the initial kick in the butt to get my experiences, observations, and lessons together into a book; and Kristen Eckstein for pulling me to the finish line. Kristen's excellent design of the insides and turning my napkin idea into the hot cover you now see certainly brought that much more polish to the project.

For early feedback and "how did we miss that" editing: Mary Anne Fagerquist, Chris Morris, Therese Sparby, and Lisbeth Tanz.

Much appreciation goes to the reviewers who shared their comments that you see in the beginning of the book and on the TakeActionReviseLater.com website.

To Adam Urbanski, for your kind words in the foreword, and for being an amazing business guru through an amazing growth period.

To Anita Johnson, whose dedication to my customers provides me with the time to create and deliver my courses and write this book.

To Scott Tousignant, Nancy Marmolejo, and Felicia Slattery for your accountability and inspiration.

To Carrie Wilkerson for your uncanny ability to send me a tweet, text message, or pick up the phone at just the right moment.

To Paulie Sabol, Donna Fox, Tom Beal, and Mike Filsaime for being the best tag-team mentors a fledgling business owner like me could have hoped for at the start.

To Ross Goldberg, Ken McArthur, David Perdew, Glen Hopkins, Mike Filsaime, and future business seminar hosts for having me teach your audiences in person.

To Lisa Benavidez and Linda Cain for helping me plan and host my workshops and seminars so smoothly.

To the charter Fast Track Masterclass members Bruce Brown, Marge Brown, Erica Cosminsky, MaryAnn D'Ambrosio, Kay Kinder, Bob Lampard, and D'vorah Lansky for allowing me to live vicariously through your amazing success and impact in the coming years!

To my colleagues, student teachers, and former students from Hammond High School for sharing your love of learning with me.

To Joanna Bartoszewicz for your love and friendship through the twists and turns of the last ten years.

And to my family members for your love and support despite time and distance between us.

Bob Jenkins

Bob Jenkins

P.S. And to you I forgot to mention, thank you for not taking it personally!

ABOUT THE AUTHOR

Bob "The Teacher" Jenkins simplifies the complex world of internet marketing into easy-to-understand lessons for business owners around the world. Where others assume you can figure it out on your own, Bob's workshops, tutorials, and coaching give you both the how-to and the why-to.

Now a full-time business coach, speaker, and internet marketing consultant, Bob is the creator of the School for Information Marketing Profits—Live Events (SIMPLE) seminars. He has published over a dozen online training courses, including the Teleseminar Formula, Discover Social Networking, and Discover Autoresponders. His IMSuccessLibrary.com is the go-to resource for learning internet marketing strategies and tools.

Prior to his success in business, Bob was an award-winning educator. For ten years, Bob taught freshmen world history and US history, as well as world religions to seniors at a public high school in Maryland. He began teaching at the school in 1997 after graduating from Florida State University with a B.A. in Social Science Education and History. He received his Master of Liberal Arts degree from Johns Hopkins University in 2006.

At the high school, Bob coached the academic team, which won the Baltimore regional championship on the It's Academic Television show in 1998 and 2006. He also coached the boys and girls tennis teams in 2007.

Bob is the President of Shylar's Quest, LLC, which began in 1999 as website design company. But his true success in business came after 2006, when he became "Bob The Teacher" and began teaching professionals and entrepreneurs around the world how to use specific internet marketing tools in their business.

Bob lives in Leland, North Carolina.

As you read this book, be sure to connect with Bob on your favorite social media channels and share your comments. Go to FollowBob.com for Twitter, Facebook, YouTube, and LinkedIn connections.

Breinigsville, PA USA
30 November 2010
250228BV00005B/1/P

9 780982 985137